Ready, Steady, Click!

The building blocks for a successful introduction to clicker training.

By

STEPHEN G. KING

Crosskeys Select Books.
London.

Ready, Steady, Click!
Crosskeys Select Books
Collier Row Road,
Romford, Essex. RM5 2BH

Authors note. I have referred to "he" rather than "she"
throughout this book. There is no reason other than to save
time, as writing he/she or it each time.

ISBN 1-903332-01-X

British Library Cataloguing
KING Stephen G.
Ready, Steady, Click!

1. Dog Training
2. Behaviour modification
3. Reinforcement (psychology)
4. Conditioned response

Preface

As this title states, this book is intended as an introduction to the scientific principles behind the process of learning. The book places an emphasis on practical solutions to behaviour problems such as those problems encountered by pet dog owners, trainers, rescue kennels, boarding kennels and pet behaviour counsellors.

Ideally this book would be of great help to those considering owning an animal, as prevention is always better than cure. However, any person whose work or daily activities involve interacting with animals whose behaviour is a problem should also benefit from reading this book. Hopefully it will also be of interest to anyone who has ever wondered about how their dog thinks and why he does some of the things (those things!) he does!

This book covers the four main principles to owning an animal:

- How to increase desirable behaviour!
- How to decrease undesirable behaviour!
- How to teach the dog what is safe to do!
- How to teach the dog what is not safe to do!

Acknowledgements

Many people helped make this book better than it would otherwise have been. I am grateful to several people who have reviewed drafts of this book and made useful comments and suggestions in particular Claire Davies MA who's detailed editorial skills and knowledge came to the fore in the final draft.

Secondly I want to pay a great tribute to three of my mentors, Robin Walker, Peter Neville and the late John Fisher whose help and encouragement paved the way for a better understanding of our canine friends.

And lastly the help and support of the godmother of clicker training, Karen Pryor who has transformed the way I now look at behaviour and planted the seed that I could write a book!

I would like to thank Josie my wife for the love and support she gave me when at times writing this book was quite a challenge. Also I would like to thank my son Chris who has been a great inspiration in encouraging me to achieve the impossible by completing this book.

Contents

Getting Ready

The Science of Behaviour Change

The task of learning any new skill or behaviour can be broken down into four distinct stages. The first stage would be unconscious incompetence. That is to say that not only do you not yet know how to do something, but that you are also unaware of it.

Take the example of learning to drive. Initially, never having driven a car you have no idea what it is like. Once you start to learn you quickly discover your limitations. You need four pairs of hands, eyes in the back of your head, and please no-one try to hold a conversation!!

Several lessons later and you are able to manage the controls, steer, coordinate the clutch, watch the road and so on. It demands all your attention, you are not yet competent, and you keep to the back roads. This is the stage of conscious incompetence when you grind the gears, over-steer and give cyclists heart attacks. Although this is uncomfortable (especially for cyclists), it is the stage when you learn the most. Next comes the stage of conscious competence. You can drive the car, but it takes all your concentration. You have learned the skill but you have not yet mastered it.

The final stage is unconscious competence. All those patterns that you have learned so painstakingly blend together into one smooth unit of behaviour. Now you can listen to the radio, take in the scenery, and hold a conversation at the same time as driving. Your conscious mind sets the outcome and leaves it to your unconscious mind to carry it out, freeing your attention for other things.

When you practice something for long enough you will reach this fourth stage and have formed solid, reliable behaviours.

Clicker training animals is no different, learning models or rules like those above are applied to an animal's behaviour in order to predict consequences and work toward increasing certain behaviours (those we like), or decreasing other behaviours (those we don't like).

Before we jump straight in and start training our best friend it may be helpful to understand the rules behind how dogs learn. Concentrate - here comes the science...

Operant and Respondent Behaviour

Clicker training works because it is founded on established scientific principles governing the learning process. When training a dog to do anything from agility, flyball, search and rescue, even just basic good dog manners involves operant behaviours.

Operant behaviour is technical terminology meaning behaviour that is influenced by the events which follow it. In other words, with operant behaviour the dog is acting on the environment as much as the environment is acting on the dog. If the dog begs and food follows, it is likely that the dog will repeat that behaviour. If a dog barks and attention follows, it is likely that the dog will repeat that behaviour. The dog learns that its behaviour has consequences.

Operant behaviours differ from respondent behaviours, which are influenced by events which precede it. These would be more reflex type behaviours. Imagine you are sitting quietly absorbed in your favourite dog magazine when a plane flying overhead breaks the sound barrier with a BOOM, and makes you jump. Not only did the noise make you jump, but there were also some physiological changes such as a temporary increase in your heart rate. This is the startle response and is an example of respondent behaviour.

In both dogs and humans unconditioned responses; the blinking of an eye when a dust particle hits it, emotions such as fear and anger, physical reactions such as sweating or shivering, have a biological basis related to survival.

The distinction between operant and respondent behaviour is sometimes confusing but behaviourists will say that respondent behaviour is elicited, whereas operant behaviour is emitted. A good example in terms of humans is the eye blink. You get a speck of dust in your eye and you blink automatically, a reflex response which would be hard to suppress. This is respondent behaviour. If, however, someone asked you to blink the request would not exert the same control as the speck of dust. You could choose whether to blink or not. A blink here would be an operant behaviour.

It is clear then that in training our dogs, in actively teaching them what it is safe to do rather than simply stopping them from doing the wrong things, in other words in employing the learning process, we will be concentrating on operant behaviour.

The process of operant conditioning, how it works, can be remembered as a simple ABC equation. In 1969 B.F. Skinner, the grandfather of behaviourism, wrote Contingencies of Reinforcement, in which he described the 'three term contingency' (contingency means something is dependent on something else). Popularly described as Antecedent > Behaviour > Consequence. Each is dependent on the other.

The antecedent, or discriminatory stimulus, is the environmental event that comes before behaviour, and could be your command or signal to your dog to act. The response is the behaviour, dog sits for example. The consequence is the resulting stimulus, dog gets food. If the consequence is pleasant then it will strengthen behaviour (Reinforcement), if unpleasant it will weaken it (Punishment). If the contingency is broken and no consequence results in an already established pattern then the relationship breaks down and extinction occurs.

When educating our furry friends in the ways of good behaviour we will do well to exploit the tools of operant behaviour: Reinforcement, Extinction, and Punishment. For the moment lets concentrate on reinforcement.

Reinforcement - accentuate the positive!

Understanding the concept of reinforcement is the keystone to understanding the learning process. Reinforcement is a similar concept to reward but is better understood as the procedure of providing pleasant consequences for behaviour. The essential difference is that rewards are defined by consensus, whereas reinforcers are defined by results.

A reward for doing well at the local exemption show might be a red rosette, but the dog owner might consider the applause and attention more reinforcing and so be motivated to enter again. In training terms it is simply what dogs like, what they will work for (positive reinforcement) as well as what they will work to avoid (negative reinforcement).

Consider these examples of reinforcement:

Duke, a 12 week old GSD is being called from the garden, he arrives in the kitchen and is presented with his food.

Duke's owners have guests visiting to see the new puppy. The visitors smile and crouch down to make themselves small. As Duke approaches, he is given lots of praise for keeping all four feet on the floor.

Paddy is a Springer Spaniel who works full time as a drug detection dog at Heathrow Airport. Paddy's duties include checking everyone's luggage before its loaded onto the plane. When Paddy was first trained if he stayed on task and completed his search, even if there were no drugs to find, his handler would give him his favourite toy and have a game with him. The positive reinforcers in these three examples are food, praise, and a toy. In each case the desired behaviour increased when the positive stimulus or consequence was presented following the behaviour.

Now consider these examples:

Gemma, a GSD, was trained to walk to heel with a check chain. When she pulled in front of her handler she received a sharp correction with the collar. After a number of repetitions she soon learned that as soon as she felt or heard her handler start to make the correction she must hurry into the heel position to avoid it.

Benny was a Springer Spaniel being trained to retrieve a dumbbell. However, Benny would refuse to take the dumbbell in his mouth. He would shut his mouth tight and refuse to give in. So Benny's handler used a common method of holding the dumbbell to his mouth and pinching the dog's ear. When Benny opened his mouth to take the dumbbell the pressure on his ear would be released.

Barney, a Golden Retriever, had been taught to sit using the 'physical prompting' technique: say 'SIT' and push the back end down into the desired position. Barney didn't like being pushed around and started to resist this happening and so extra force was used to position the dog. After a number of repetitions Barney obeyed the command in order to avoid this over-handling, learning that the word 'SIT' was his opportunity to avoid being pushed around.

You can see that these examples of negative reinforcement involve aversives, in other words things that the dog will avoid or escape if given the choice. These examples should also illustrate that negative reinforcement is not the same as punishment, which is a consequence (or stimulus) that would decrease behaviour.

It must be remembered that reinforcement is the consequence for increasing behaviour. In order to use negative reinforcement you must be willing to expose your dog to an ongoing aversive stimulus. To put it bluntly, you must be willing to harm your dog (or at least make him reasonably uncomfortable) until he complies with what you want him to do. Once the dog performs the behaviour you remove the aversive.

The removal of pain, or discomfort, is a very reinforcing event and should increase the probability of the behaviour it follows. When removing the aversive timing is very important. If it is not removed at the exact moment the dog complies, the dog will not make the association between the behaviour and the relief from pain or discomfort. There are such aversive apparatus as electric shock collars that are designed to be used as a negative reinforcer and are fashionable in certain dog circles. On a personal note, I detest the use of devices that shock dogs or inflict pain when there are solutions that are much better for the relationship between dog and owner.

Primary Reinforcers

As well as having positive or negative reinforcers we can also divide reinforcement into primary or secondary.

A primary reinforcer is a stimulus that motivates your dog and for which it is prepared to work. Primary reinforcers are those which are immediately reinforcing and are simply reinforcing as a result of the dog's evolution as a species. These can include food, water, sexual stimulation, foraging, sniffing / scenting, attention, grooming, coolness (when body temperature is high), and warmth (when the body temperature is low).

As these examples suggest, primary reinforcers often have to do with biological processes. Each dog will value some reinforcers over others and each will have a relative value which varies from day to day, and moment to moment. Some reinforcers are not immediately obvious, for instance if you were a dog restrained in your home and cannot move about or get out, the chance of freedom can be very reinforcing.

Many dogs have breed specific behaviours that are pre-wired such as the Springer Spaniel who is visually orientated and seem distracted by anything that moves in the air, such as a leaf falling from a tree. The Border Collie likes to herd and chase joggers, motor bikes, things that move across the ground. Owners of such dogs often wonder why their dog is not paying attention in an outdoor training class, despite having his favourite treat that he works so well for at home. For this dog food cannot compete with a field of birds or a herd of sheep on the move.

We can evaluate your dog's preferences by using a canine reinforcement analysis. Successful trainers experiment with a variety of reinforcers, so that for dogs that are people oriented attention might be a big payoff. For those dogs that are 'chow hounds' food and treats may be the answer. Dogs that prefer praise or squeaky toys need to be catered for. The touch sensitive dog would like to be stroked or scratched on different parts of his anatomy, and lastly the social/competitive type might work for a ball game, tug or any game with a high calorific burn up! With each of these types we could have a list of the dog's order of preferences under these headings:

- Food - list your dog's favourite food/treats.
- Play - List ways your dog enjoys playing with you.
- Praise - Words that you use when interacting with your dog.
- Touch - List your dog's favourite petting/touching/scratching spots.

Taking touch as an example we could describe it in a number of ways:
- Location - chest, tummy, ears, top of head, tail, feet.
- Pressure - hard, soft.
- Texture - scratch with fingers, flat of hand, stroke.
- Duration - how long it lasts.
- Movement - shaping patterns.

Find out what your dog likes! (For more information read The Tellington Touch, by Linda Tellington-Jones, a book that comes highly recommended.)

Once you have listed the reinforcers that work for your dog in each section, further categorise by selecting the favourite in order of priority for each heading. Analysis of this sort should be carried out to determine the likes and dislikes rather than assuming something is a reinforcer.

Breed differences, learning histories, and specific environmental and physical conditions all play a part in detecting which stimuli will work as reinforcers for a particular dog. The effectiveness of a reinforcer is often described in terms of motivation, deprivation, and satiation.

Motivation is at the heart of reinforcement. If the dog is not motivated to do something the event cannot be a reinforcer. Take, for example, offering a piece of carrot to a dog who dislikes carrots.

Deprivation occurs when a reinforcer becomes more powerful after the dog has gone for a period of time without it. Such an example would be a dog who is more interested in food when it has missed a meal.

Satiation occurs when the dog has had enough of a particular reinforcer, making it less effective. If a puppy is fed at 8.00am before going to puppy training at 11.00am, the appetite for motivation will have lost some of its appeal.

Secondary Reinforcers

Secondary reinforcers are dependent on their association with other reinforcers. They acquire their reinforcing powers by being paired a number of times with an established reinforcer. In other words they are learned. If you show a deaf dog a thumbs up signal and then provide a treat, then the thumbs up signal will become reinforcing. Verbal praise is the most commonly used secondary reinforcer. When you say "good dog" and present food, or a pat on the head, the dog learns to associate praise with a primary reinforcer. Praise becomes a secondary reinforcer.

Secondary reinforcers are also called conditioned reinforcers. This is because of their dependency on a learned association taking place. The process by which neutral events become reinforcing is known by scientists as classical or Pavlovian conditioning, after well known experiments conducted by Ivan Pavlov (1849 - 1936).

Pavlov observed that the dogs he was studying would salivate before food was placed in their mouths. He began to suspect that the dogs were associating the arrival of the laboratory assistants, or the sound of the door opening with food. He began to test his theory by ringing a bell just before feeding the dogs. After a number of trials, the ringing of the bell alone caused the dogs to salivate.

The dogs were displaying learned associations. Salivation, in Pavlov's model, becomes a conditioned response, stimulated by the previously neutral, but now learned (or conditioned) stimulus. We can use this process to our advantage in training. You can see how we have a method of turning neutral things such as sounds or signals into powerful and useful reinforcers. Our dogs already do this. For example, initially a lead presented to a puppy means absolutely nothing, but after a few trips to the park it will become a secondary reinforcer. A lead means walks, car keys means a car ride to get a walk, a tin opener opening a can means food is on its way. When Dad puts his coat on and finds the lead its walk time. In the process the coat becomes a secondary reinforcer. Secondary reinforcers are less susceptible to satiation. If you have ever been complimented many times, a compliment is still likely to be reinforcing.

So if a noise can become a reinforcer think how useful that will be for training. Anyone who has seen dolphin trainers at work might have noticed that they use whistles as conditioned reinforcers. A whistle means "you've got it right". When the animal trainers blow a whistle to let the dolphin know that his performance is correct the trainers are able to offer reinforcement from a distance.

In this way a conditioned reinforcer is also known as a bridging stimulus (slang term), as it buys you time to get the primary reinforcer (fish) to the dolphin. Other animal trainers and dog trainers have started to use the clicker in the same way as the dolphin trainers use the whistle.

So what Is a clicker?

A clicker is a child's toy that trainers have decided to use to reinforce an animal's behaviour. The clicker is a small metal and plastic device that makes a double clicking sound.

Using a clicker instead of your voice gives us a tool that makes a unique sound that has never been heard before and usually doesn't have any pre-existing associations.

The signal is consistent, and deliverable with precision and from a distance. So use of the clicker allows your dog to learn that whatever behaviour causes a click will be reinforced, useful information to the dog as it predicts the availability of a reinforcer so that the behaviour is likely to be repeated. Behaviour is a function of its consequences. It is also an event marker - the click marks the behaviour as it occurs. The click also marks the end of the behaviour, and you are now ready to start again.

Clicker training has another good effect on the more experienced dog, the sound of the first click becomes a context marker, or to put it informally, it tells the dog the training "game" is on and that there is a chance of reinforcement. When the clicks eventually stop, (extinction is also applied) your dog will know that the "game" has finished. What clicker training can also achieve for your dog is a change in motivation,

which can result in a confidence boost!
Using reinforcement

There is no procedure more important in dog training than reinforcement. It is worth taking the time to describe some basic rules for using reinforcement effectively:

1. Define the target behaviour.
Its best to literally write down a brief description of the behaviour or set of behaviours that would qualify for reinforcement (i.e. a behaviour that if increased would benefit the dog and owner). In puppies you could aim for lengthening their attention span, for example.
2. Choose the appropriate reinforcers.
Before you can reinforce target behaviour, you have to choose one or more reinforcers. The most important thing to remember is never to use negative reinforcers if positive reinforcers are available. The second thing to remember is that positive reinforcers are always available. Conditioned reinforcers such as a clicker paired with some tasty food, or a clicker paired with a chew tug game will be just the job for increasing that desired behaviour.
3. Make the reinforcement immediate and certain (click and treat).
Using a clicker allows you to mark the behaviour just as it happens. The more closely that reinforcement follows the target behaviour the more likely it is to be effective. Any delay in delivering the signal may result in the wrong behaviours being reinforced. For example, puppy sits and you click and treat. If you delay the chances are that the puppy has stood up, scratched, barked, or otherwise added some unwanted behaviour. By certain I refer to the fact that the more likely the target behaviour is to result in reinforcement the more rapidly the behaviour is to increase in strength. In other words the best results are usually obtained when reinforcement is almost certain to occur when the target behaviour occurs, but is unlikely to occur otherwise.
4. Observe the results
Observing the results is an essential part of the training process. Learning to perceive the difference that makes the difference. Learning to observe your dog, when to reinforce or not, and when to raise your criteria will become easier with time and experience. As will, most importantly, having the patience to allow your dog to work through these procedures so that it will heighten your dog's performance and improve his creativity for learning.

Learning to perceive the difference that makes the difference is known as the "art of reinforcement" and the only way of achieving fantastic results is to go out and do it, as reading about it doesn't give the practice that you require.

I would suggest finding a training partner who can observe your performance and give you general guidance with your timing and movement around your dog.

Try clicking one of your family with their movements, the goal behaviour for example would be to get the clicks right on target. Click somebody walking, clicking when his or her left foot hits the ground, and then try the right foot. Have a friend bounce a ball and you have to click just as the ball hits the ground, then click when the ball is half way up from the bounce, and see how many you can get on target. Try throwing the ball onto a wall some distance from you and try to click just as the ball hits the wall, this will help for distance work, as getting the timing right is crucial.

Take it steady

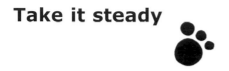

Getting Started

Most dogs readily take to clicker training as free food, toys, or some other nice thing are paired with this unique sound. Once you have decided what your dog likes and will work for (you have chosen your reinforcer/s) you are ready to 'power up' your clicker.

For a successful FIRST training session where you will introduce your dog to the clicker for the first time, its best to choose a nice quiet location in a room with no distractions.

Start by getting your clicker and around 30 to 50 pieces of your dog's favourite reinforcer cut into small thumbnail size pieces. For a Tibetan terrier this is good news, but if you have a adult Irish Wolfhound give several thumbnail-sized bits at once so that he knows it is worthwhile.

It is best to keep the environment stress-free and quiet, which means it is also wise to remove any other dog or other animal from the room being used.

The process of conditioning your dog to the clicker (creating that learned association) is relatively easy. Click first, then treat immediately after. Do not 'muddy the water' by talking so as to distract the dog from learning the click-signal-treat association. If the food is in your hand place it on a nearby table and if your dog looks at the food = no click, when he looks at you = click!

You can condition your dog to the fact that if the food is not present he can make it reappear and cause a click. The sooner this early lesson is taught to the dog the better as it is the click which is more important not the food. He will then work out that even if the reinforcer is hidden, by performing behaviour, he can make it reappear. This way he thinks he's training you!

At this stage do not try to ask for any specific behaviours. Repeat procedure in a number of short sessions throughout the day and when your dog is pricking his ears when he hears the click you know he is getting the message. You can test if your dog has made the association by clicking when he is not paying attention and watch his reaction, you should see him become alert and come to you for his treat.

A number of dogs that are sound sensitive may display an initial fear reaction to the sound of the clicker. In such a case this can be overcome by desensitising this signal by placing the clicker in your pocket to produce a muffled sound, or find an oven glove and click from inside, or try clicking from another room while your dog is eating.

You may want to use a pen top which makes a similar but softer noise. If your dog has an unpleasant reaction you should still persist in finding a conditioned reinforcer such as a whistle as it is the key to using operant conditioning techniques.

Once the conditioning process is complete you have a wonderful tool to communicate with your dog to teach what is safe to do and what is not safe to do!

Getting the Behaviour We Want

You want me to do what?

In order to really start training we need to have some behaviour to reinforce. There are three ways of approaching this. We can either shape or prompt a behaviour, or we can use a combination of the two. They differ slightly, if we are being strictly technical, in that shaping tends to concentrate on a 'hands off' approach, waiting for the animal to offer behaviour freely. This makes it a useful way (sometimes the only way) of training fearful or aggressive animals, even wildlife.

Prompting involves some kind of outside influence. A good trainer will recognise which to use in any given situation, often depending on the dog's learning history, and what it is likely to do as a natural behaviour or response. Shaping is usually more suitable for working a natural behaviour, such as laying down or barking.

Although these are equally amenable to prompting if circumstances make it more appropriate. Whereas prompting is undoubtedly more useful in moulding more novel behaviours.

It is worth looking at these in more detail to understand what is meant by them and how to use them in our clicker training.

Shaping

Free shaping is a concept of training where the dog is allowed to move freely in any manner that it desires. From the behaviours offered, the trainer has to click the behaviours that he would like to see repeated or a behaviour that needs to be refined. The behaviour has to be captured as the dog is performing it. If you have previously watched your dog/puppy move around the room that you have decided to train in, you will notice that most behaviour that we need for obedience is already available for us to reinforce. The dog most likely will sit, lay down, stand, come to us, and move away from us, quite instinctively.

Pick a behaviour for which the dog has already a pre-existing tendency such as laying down. Be seated with a cup of coffee and a magazine with some food on the side and your clicker at the ready. Totally ignore your dog until the predicted behaviour has occurred, then click and treat. Before he trots over to get his treat, throw the food to him. If he comes over totally ignore him and wait until he goes away to any part of the room and settles in to the down position. What you are in fact doing is training your dog at some distance to "lay down" without any cues or commands.

Used in this way to mould one whole target behaviour the process is relatively straight forward. But we can also shape whole behaviours by reinforcing parts of the whole, or each small step towards the complete behaviour. This is known as shaping by successive approximations. Using this approach you would reinforce anything your dog does which resembles the target behaviour to some degree. An important characteristic of behaviour is its variability; we never do anything the same way twice. It is this fact that makes shaping possible. The first step in shaping is to decide what behaviour is to be "shaped".

What is it that you want the dog to be doing at the end of the shaping procedure? As you look for variations that are closer approximations to the target behaviour, you reinforce those variations (C/T). Some of the new behaviour will be in the direction you want the behaviour to go and can be reinforced (C/T).

Perhaps the best rule of thumb to follow to reinforce an approximation several times or until a closer approximation has appeared, which-ever comes first. If no new approximation has appeared after several reinforcements, withhold reinforcement until a new approximation occurs. Shaping is as much an art as it is a science and there are no clear cut guide lines to follow concerning when to raise the requirements for reinforcement, or how much to raise them.

As a practical example, which you might like to try, you might want your dog to "spin". To get to the target behaviour, we have to have a very clear idea of what it is. Our successive approximation list might look something like this.

- Click for any head turn to the left.
- Click for head turn to the left until dog offers it, freely and at will.
- Withhold the click for the head turn, to get more

than just a head turn.
- Click only for head turn with some shoulder movement.
- Withhold click for more turn than that.
- Click only for head and full shoulder turn.
- Withhold click for head, shoulder turn-wanting foot movement.
- Click for head/shoulder turn with foot movement.
- Withhold click for head/shoulder/and foot movement-wanting more steps.
- Click for steps taken to the left with head/shoulder movements.
- Withhold click for steps taken to the left following head turn-wanting half spin.
- Click for dog turning half spin.
- Withhold click for dog turning more than half spin.
- Click for more than half turn.
- Withhold click for more turn than above.
- Click for dog turning more than half way round.
- Withhold click for more than that.
- Click for three quarter spin.
- Withhold click for more than three quarter spin.
- Click for the complete spin.

In general, shaping progresses more rapidly when the increases in the requirements for reinforcement are small. When you hold out for a better performance, the better performance should be only a very slight improvement. If a big advance in performance appears, reinforce it (C/T); but do not hold out for big advances. Remember if you look after the pennies, the pounds look after themselves. (A lot of small improvements add up to one big improvement).

You have to make judgements about when to raise your requirements and by how much, and sometimes you will be wrong. If you err on the side of prudence, reinforcing behaviour at a given step more often than is necessary and making very small increases in the requirements for reinforcement, the worst that is likely to happen is that progress will be slow. If you make the mistake of moving too quickly, then progress will stop and you may see some strong emotional reactions. If you expect too much from the dog and the behaviour breaks down you can drop your requirements to a previous level where you were both succeeding.

Obviously, you want to make progress towards the target behaviour, but if you get stalled you will need to take a back step in order to go forward again. If you find yourself having to back step numerous times, it's a pretty good bet that your requirements for reinforcement are too high.

The only way you can measure how successful you are at shaping behaviour is by noting what changes in the behaviour are occurring. Are you seeing the improvement towards the target behaviour? Is the behaviour that occurs now closer to the target behaviour than previously? Is it time to hold out for a closer approximation of the target behaviour? Has the behaviour begun to break down? Should you take a back step? These are the questions you must ask while you are shaping. You can only answer these questions if you are paying close attention to changes in the behaviour.

Remember that so long as you are reinforcing closer approximations to the target behaviour, you are making steady progress, so when it comes to approximations, remember to think small.

Prompting

What we are going to concentrate on at this point are the physical, modelling, and environmental prompts that we can employ to target and mould behaviour in the right direction.

There are also verbal prompts (cues or commands), and gesture prompts (such as hand signals), and we will talk about these later as they are generally, though not always, reserved for getting the behaviour after it has been learned. In other words for putting the behaviour under stimulus control.

Although it is worth mentioning here that, especially with gesture prompts in the form of facial cues, or hand movements that sometimes we can unintentionally prompt our dogs. This is what psychologists call superstitious behaviour. Lots of dogs that I have worked with continually keep looking for additional body language. Often we are not aware of these more subtle prompts, but they can seriously confuse the learning process if we are not conscious of their occurring and we must be mindful of the whole picture according to the dog's eyes.

Physical prompts are achieved by actually handling the animal, such as pushing the back end down for the sit behaviour. A further example is guiding the dog with a lead or collar to go over a Long Jump.

Another way of prompting a behaviour is to demonstrate or model it. Teaching the dog to jump over a low hurdle when you go over first and the dog follows behind on the lead. Dog training instructors will describe behaviour to be taught, demonstrate with their own dog (model), and then help you to emulate that procedure of learning which you go away and practice.

Environmental prompts are those prompts where you add or remove something. Such as the Target Touch Stick, plastic lids, or a square piece of card. In agility I remember the technique used for training my dog Emma to negotiate the weaving poles at a fast rate of knots. I used wire placed strategically around the weaving poles so as to form a channel. You can now buy these items from a good agility equipment supplier. Some dogs as they get older find climbing stairs quite difficult, so a good environmental prompt would be to build a ramp just like the ones built for older people.

We will use these different types of prompts in different guises for some of the training examples later in the book.

Targeting

Targeting is a basic foundation skill for teaching all kinds of behaviour that your dog needs to know. It is useful in house training, any obedience application, including 'walk with me', road safety and much more. Targeting gives you the ability to teach complex or novel behaviours much more easily. Teaching your dog to 'go out' from you, retrieve, recognise objects by name, close doors, open doors and switch lights on and off are some of the behaviours that are achievable.

Using your hand as a target is a great behaviour to teach any age of dog, especially young puppies and even older dogs. We need to teach at the earliest opportunity that a moving hand on or about the dog is an acceptable behaviour. We need to be able to check the dog all over and of course the Veterinary Surgeon will need to be able to check your furry friend from top to tail if he is going to do his job well.

It is worth mentioning that playing rough and tumble games where the dog is encouraged to 'mouth' and 'grab bite' anyone can often lead to some serious consequences later on and is best avoided.

Our target behaviour is to shape the dog to touch your hand with his nose. Hold your hand slightly above the dog's nose and a little to one side, a few inches away. Now keep perfectly still and wait, if he glances at it C/T. Many dogs will naturally investigate and sniff a persons hand so as your dog investigates by sniffing, or as his nose touches or nearly touches your hand, C/T. Make sure you capture this just as it happens. Once your dog's interest in touching has increased move your hand to the other side of your dog's nose and repeat procedure at least five times.

When shaping your hand, as a target be careful how you hold your hand as if this is similar to any hand signal that the dog already knows, you may then confuse your dog. Having said that once the dog understands that touching your hand consistently and reliably will earn a C/T, you can use this behaviour to teach SIT, DOWN, and STAND.

Step 1. To start the sit behaviour, while the dog is standing up, hold your hand at nose level as though you have a treat in your hand. Now lift your hand up and back (towards his tail), so he has to follow your hand. If he offers any crouching movement C/T.

Traditionally trainers would go for the whole behaviour in one go, but clicker trainers have the option of shaping by successive approximation and so we can also reinforce any small movements that are in the desired target range. This means we can give the dog a clue to what we want and aim towards it in small steps if this is what the dog offers us.

Repeat procedure and wait a second or two and C/T any improvements. After a couple of repetitions you should have the whole behaviour. If not be patient, take your hand away and then try again.

Do not be tempted to push the dog or tell it what to do (you cannot trigger a behaviour if he doesn't know what to do)

If the dog is jumping up, your hand is probably too high. Concentrate on keeping the hand target just a few inches from your dog's head. If the dog persists with this excitable behaviour, remove your hand and keep perfectly still and wait until this behaviour has died down. When the dog puts four feet back on the ground we start the shaping again. Now try again by placing your hand at nose height, now lift your hand up and back and you're dog should try and follow your hand with its nose. You are targeting the dog into folding its back legs into a sit. Click and treat when the backside touches the ground, the click "marks" the behaviour you want. Make sure that you give the treat immediately afterwards, give it at nose height so as not to tempt jumping up. We do not worry what the dog is doing as we feed, the click tells them the behaviour is over and they are free to move to get the treat. Shape the behaviour a few more times using your hand as a target, after every sit, C/T.

Step 2. Now we can increase the length of time that the dog will sit. Use your hand to target the sit, when he is sitting withhold the click, to a count of 5 seconds, click and treat if he is still sitting. Target the sit using your hand, remove your hand and place to your side. Is he still sitting? If so, C/T. If not, repeat targeting, remove hand, if the dog remains sitting, C/T.

By delaying the click a little you are teaching the dog to sit and stay until he hears the click. This time delay in the click can be built up to about a couple minutes in about a week quite easily. Keep training 'short and sweet'. Four or five minute sessions, two to three times a day will get you the best results, without pain and stress.

You will find it quite astonishing at the amount of learning that takes place between training sessions. If you find a problem today that troubles you, it might well work itself out by tomorrow.

Step 3. As soon as the dog is sitting for a few seconds without your hand as a target, you can start to use it for the down behaviour. You should find the hand target can easily be taught as a prompt for down.

Hold your hand at your dog's nose as in the sit position, i.e. as if holding a treat, this time with the palm facing down. Then move it down, slowly, between the dog's front paws, very close to the dog. The nose will follow the hand and you can C/T any movements in the desired target range.

As an example you could C/T for any of these progressive movements towards the desired behaviour:

- When the front leg/s bend at the elbow.
- When the front foot moves forward.
- When both feet move forward.
- When the elbows touch the ground.
- When you get the whole behaviour.
- Eventually the back end flops down to the floor, C/T.

Repeat this procedure a couple of times so that he has the idea. Then do the same as before, but this time as the hand touches the floor and the dog lays down, pull your hand away to the side, if the dog is still lying down, C/T.

If the dog gets up after the click, that's fine. Start again and repeat the procedure.

Training note: If you are heading for the obedience competition ring, you may want to start the down behaviour from the standing position, not from the sit position, as this helps the dog to be properly placed.

Step 4. At some point (and this would be when you felt you could bet money on the behaviour) start to reduce the hand targeting movement to the floor. Wait a few moments to see if your dog will attempt the down ON HIS OWN.

Reinforce any movements for the desired behaviour without targeting. Work to the same criteria that you used before with the hand target communicate to your dog that he is on the right track! Let the clicker do the talking! Repeat and watch the dog. You may actually see the moment when the 'lightbulb' goes on, the moment that the dog has learned that by giving this behaviour he will earn a C/T. That's when your dog will start to throw this behaviour at you and start to down on purpose.

The dog may even hurl himself to the floor. When the dog has learnt that it is his behaviour that makes you click and that he can earn his treats, he thinks he is training you!

This is an important first lesson, as learning how to learn is an integral part of operant conditioning.

Step 5. Teaching the stand from the sit position is a snip! Target sit, no click. Place you're hand two inches from the dogs nose, move hand, at waist level slowly away from nose, C/T any back-end movement, just as the behaviour happens. You do not want the whole dog moving just the back end. Repeat procedure and then click for faster behaviour, ignore slow movements.

Step 6. To keep the training program interesting and to make progress, you need to keep adding to your requirements for clicks. We could introduce a new criteria to extend the duration, time (stay) in the position, speed, distance, position of behaviour, add distractions, teach a hand signal, add a cue and even go out of sight.

Training notes: Start a new training session with a review.

It is always a good suggestion to start each session by going back a step or two. If you got to step six or five go back to step four and review the behaviour that was being achieved and shape the behaviour back up to step six.

Fading the Prompt

Now you see it, now you don't!

The only drawback with using prompts is that unless you want to be using them forever then you have to fade them out. With the agility weaving pole example, using wires works well for beginning dogs but the dog must eventually be able to work without special prompts. Trainers who use wire prompts to teach the weave gradually close the wires to get the perfect weave and then start to remove one wire at a time until the dog is weaving without any special help.

As with reinforcement, there are some basic rules which we can follow to ensure that we are using prompting and fading to our best advantage.

1. Define the target behaviour.
   You should identify the prompts that will produce the behaviour and have a plan to fade them.
2. Choose suitable prompts.
   Remember how we used our hand as a target to teach the down behaviour?
3. Maintain (reinforce) the behaviour before gradually fading the prompt.

Prompts should be faded so gradually that mistakes are less likely to occur, and a simple rule to apply is to continue reinforcing with a prompt until the behaviour occurs reliably and without hesitation. That is, as Gary Wilkes the behaviourist puts it, until you would bet $20 that the dog will perform the behaviour. Then you are ready to reduce the prompt strength which when faded gradually will give the dog what we call errorless learning. When teaching the down behaviour start to reduce the hand targeting movement to the floor. Wait a few moments to see if your dog will attempt the down ON HIS OWN.

4. Observe the results.

Are you fading the prompt too quickly? If you reduce the prompt too much the target behaviour may not occur. Prompting and fading are in essence easy procedures, but they are not that easy that nothing can go wrong.

Chaining

If we want to train a target behaviour that is quite complex, a retrieve for example, sometimes it is easier to see it and to train it as a set, or chain, of individual behaviour steps. This is what we call chaining and is the process by which we condition, or train, a behaviour chain. A behaviour chain is simply a sequence of related behaviours, each of which provides the cue for the next, and the last of which produces the reinforcer.

Practically every behaviour we teach a dog has a behaviour chain. Some chains end up with one or two cues like the retrieve and other behaviour chains have lots of cues/prompts such as agility. Whether you are training simple behaviours or something more complex, each step in the behaviour chain serves as a cue for the next behaviour until ultimately you reinforce (C/T) the last behaviour in that chain.

There are two types of chaining, forward and reverse. The elements must be taught in a logical sequence, chaining either forward or backward. As its name suggests, forward chaining starts with the first task in the chain. When the dog can perform the first element reliably, you have the dog perform the first and second elements and reinforce (C/T) this effort. Notice that you start at the beginning of the chain and proceed to the second element and when performed reliably move onto the third task and reinforce.

Reverse chaining obviously starts with the last task. Chaining backwards often results in the best results. This is because by teaching the end behaviour first and adding a new behaviour in front of that and then in front of that one, the dog has more certainty about when he gets his reinforcement. He has to perform all the other behaviours before he gets to that one that has always paid off in the past. In forward training a lot of the dogs certainty of reinforcement is lost through the chaining process. An obedience dog that has been clicker trained for a behaviour by reverse chaining often seems to find the opportunity to perform an 'end' behaviour reinforcing in itself. This is why you find some that enjoy a 'finish' so much that they do it with real flourish.

Of course we can apply some rules we can follow when shaping a behaviour chain:

1. Define the target behaviour.

To teach a dog the basic retrieve, as an example, you need to work out how many components there are in the chain. So you need to visualise the whole behaviour and write down each one. The procedure of breaking a task into smaller steps is called task analysis. For the retrieve the task analysis could read:

- R1. Wait for the throw and the cue to retrieve.
- R2. Go immediately and undeviating to the dumbbell.
- R3. Pick up the dumbbell without hesitation, mouthing, or dropping.
- R4. Return directly to the handler
- R5. Return in the 'present' position
- R6. Wait for 'give' cue
- R7. Finish in heel position

Once you are clear in your own mind as to what elements of the chain need to be built you can move on.

2. Reinforce successive elements of the chain.

First, of course, you will need to get an element to appear, and this will require shaping. In most cases each link will need to be shaped up. When you have shaped up one element and reinforced it, you then move on to the next. You continue shaping and reinforcing elements until all the components have been mastered. What you learn in a chain is that it is not just the number of tasks, but to perform those tasks in the right order. You can either start at the beginning of a chain and work your way to the end, or you can accomplish the same thing with reverse chaining, in which case you start at the end and work backwards.

3. Observe the results.

Each element of the chain should be being performed solidly and reliably before moving onto the next link in the chain. With careful monitoring of the results you will be able to make these judgements. Never be too eager to rush the process, as a step by step approach by you will certainly be reinforced by the results you get from your dog.

Confirmed Pullers v Behaviour Chains.

Most real pullers who charge off like a train in front of you have actually been trained to pull forward by their owners constantly pulling back or at worst keeping the lead tight. Every step taken with a tight lead reinforces that behaviour. If you have a dog that is a confirmed puller, it may be that there is a chain of events which reinforce each behaviour as it happens. Let's start in the home, the lead is initially a neutral stimulus, which when paired with a walk becomes a conditioned stimulus for excitement. We fight and struggle with the dog to get his lead on, he pulls us to the door. He pulls us through the door to get to the path. As we walk down the road each step we take with a tight lead with him pulling reinforces this behaviour.

The last behaviour in this chain is getting to the park, very reinforcing. All those nice sniffs, new people and friendly dogs to play with, especially when the dog is let off the lead, he gets this as a 'jackpot'.

Break the Chain.

So there is more going on than just pulling, we need to break the chain of events. We will look at 'sit and have your collar felt' and 'coming when called' a bit later, so for now lets work on simply getting your dog to walk beside you on a loose lead. The motivation for the dog to pull could be getting to the park, so we need to reverse this situation so that there are less reinforcers at work to keep the dog pulling.

Step 1. Place the dog in the car and drive a short distance away from your house. About 60 metres is a good distance at which to start. Place the dog on the pavement and use the double training lead. Begin walking back towards your house, (after locking up your car!). Click every two or three steps, stopping to treat. If your dog lags behind do not pull him just loosen the lead a little and wait until he moves toward you, C/T. Resist the urge to pull him behind you, this will only make him brace himself against the pressure you are exerting on the lead and pull backwards from you. If he surges ahead do not pull against him.

Stop and stand still, the dog needs to learn that nothing happens when the lead becomes tight. When the dog moves near you and the lead loosens, C/T. As your dog gets the hang of what is desired you can begin to increase the distance you walk back home.

When you are confident that your dog is walking without pulling then you can walk him from home to your car, parked a short distance from your house. After this has been accomplished you can walk him out and back from his exercise area where he can be allowed some free running exercise.

Step 2. Over many walks you can increase the level of stimulation. Let the dog realise that when he pulls on the lead, nothing happens; but if the lead is loose, you will move toward the other dog, the new person, that interesting lamp post, or whatever he wants to investigate. Your dog will then learn to take the responsibility for keeping a loose lead and with time will become a pleasure to take out.

Stop Gap Measure.

The Gentle Leader is a sort of halter for dogs, like a halter for horses. (See Crosskeys Select books). It goes round the nose and neck. The lead fastens under the jaw. The dog can still open its mouth comfortably; this is not a muzzle. However if the dog pulls, its head is turned back towards the handler and it cannot see where it is going, so it stops pulling. You do not need to do any training at all. Just hold the lead and walk along. The dog may fight the collar at first, just like puppies fight a normal collar for the first time, but it will teach itself to keep a loose lead. This is an excellent temporary fix while you are retraining the dog, or it can be used as a permanent help to a frail owner or a child who must walk a big dog.

Stimulus Discrimination
and Stimulus Control

When you learn to drive a car you have to learn to press three pedals (unless you have an automatic), not all at the same time! Applying too much pressure to the accelerator pedal when you approach traffic lights that have turned red can have very negative results, even fatal consequences.

Learning to drive a car means learning to drive a car under certain circumstances and also learning to avoid performing those acts under other circumstances. When to use the brake and how much pressure. When to use the accelerator, when to use the clutch and accelerator in unison. Behaviour tends to have different frequencies in different situations. The tendency for behaviour to occur in one situation and not in another, is called stimulus discrimination.

Remembering back to our A>B>C equation for operant conditioning you will recall that Antecedents are the stimuli that come before Behaviour. So an antecedent, or discrimination stimulus, could also be described as any event in the presence of which target behaviour is likely to have consequences that affect its frequency.

In the case of Alex the Labrador, for example, begging for food at the table, the antecedents would be the food and the family present at the table. The behaviour following these antecedents was begging and the consequences were that Alex was being reinforced with food. Later, when the family wanted to change Alex's behaviour, the consequence became the family ignoring the dog for begging (a process known as extinction, discussed later).

Since the consequences associated with a discrimination stimulus can either strengthen or weaken behaviour, it follows that there are two kinds of discriminative stimuli.

S^D: an event in the presence of which the target behaviour is reinforced

S^Δ: An event in the presence of which the target behaviour is not reinforced. S^Δ stands for S delta which is the Greek letter D.

When behaviour is reinforced only in the presence of a particular antecedent stimulus (cue), stimulus control develops as a result.

An S^D is a discriminative stimuli that signals the availability of reinforcement. For example the cue 'sit' while the dog is standing, is S^D

for the dog to sit, while also S$^\Delta$ for the dog to stand. An S^D (cue) is said to set the occasion for a particular behaviour and no other behaviours are called for in the presence of that S^D (cue).

In competitive obedience competition, there is an exercise called scent discrimination in which the dog has to go out and retrieve a scent cloth. The exercise differs slightly depending on the test (A, B, or C).In test A and B the dog only has to find the handler's scent and in class C the dog has to discriminate between the judge's scent on a cloth, and from both decoy and neutral cloths. We can use stimulus discrimination to shape this behaviour.

After initially teaching the dog to retrieve all sorts of articles including cloth one at a time, you are ready to teach discrimination. With tongs place one neutral cloth (no scent) on the floor in the scent area, then allow your dog to sniff the scent cloth in your hand. Give the dog the sit cue and then place the scent cloth parallel with the neutral cloth but one foot away, then return to the dog and send him to find the scent article by giving him the retrieve cue.

In this case the scent article is S^D and the neutral article is S$^\Delta$. If the dog correctly retrieves the scent cloth, reinforcement is forthcoming if the dog retrieves the neutral cloth, reinforcement is withheld. (S$^\Delta$ are related to the extinction process or what's known as a non-reinforcement signal).

In case you hadn't noticed, we have come all this way without giving the dog a command of any kind! How do we get the dog to do what we want when we want it? Understanding how to use antecedent stimuli is crucial to the training process because it is the way we get target behaviour under stimulus control, or happening when we want it to happen! We say behaviour is under "stimulus control" when discrimination training has been effective.

This is when the dog produces the behaviour reliably on cue, does not produce the behaviour when not cued, and does not offer anything other than the correct behaviour for that particular cue. We have just been talking about a dog that recognises a particular cue as S^D for a particular behaviour and S$^\Delta$ for all other behaviour. The aim of training is to establish stimulus control over all known behaviours, which are solid and reliable.

Clicker trainers first establish (shape) the behaviour and when the behaviour is solid and reliable (you could bet money on it) we add a cue. The cue may be given just before the behaviour happens, the dog responds and reinforcement is forthcoming.

To establish a cue to behaviour there are four aspects to consider. The first two are like traffic lights, green for 'go' and red for 'no-go'. What this means in real terms is that the behaviour has to be extinguished in the absence of the conditioned stimulus (cue). This does not mean the dog has to stand up all day unless you say "down" or "sit", these rules only apply when the dog is in a working or training situation. At other times the dog is free to do what it pleases. The other thing to consider when teaching a dog to learn the meaning of cues is that they have to learn to wait for a cue.

Ensuring that the behaviour is occurring frequently, you say "sit" and reinforce that response. Wait a few moments and let a "sit" or two go unreinforced. Then you say "sit" get a response and then reinforce. You are in the same training session, reinforcing on cue "sits" and extinguishing off-cue sits. Withhold cues from half a second to a second and so on until the dog is visibly attending to you waiting for the cue.

There are four criteria to establishing stimulus control. Each one of these criteria needs to be worked on, one at a time as separate training tasks.

1. The behaviour always occurs immediately upon presentation of the conditioned stimulus - When you say "sit" the dog sits

2. The behaviour should never occur in the absence of the stimulus (in working mode)
3. The behaviour should never occur in response to some other stimulus -when you say "down" the dog should not offer the "sit" instead.
4. No other behaviour should occur in response to this stimulus - When you say "sit" the dog does not respond by lying down and barking or leaping up at you to lick your face. One cue = one behaviour.

When all four criteria are met and only then, does the dog really understand thoroughly and conclusively the cue "sit". Some practical examples which demonstrate how to add the cue are in the next chapter, see in particular conditioning the Target Touch Stick.

Incidentally to establish a second cue for a learned behaviour is called transferring the stimulus control. To make a transfer, you present the new stimulus, or cue (perhaps a verbal command like "sit") first, then add the old cue (which might be a hand signal) and then reinforce the response. Gradually fade the old stimulus so that the dog pays attention to the new stimulus until the response is given equally well to the new stimulus, even when the old stimulus is not given at all.

This procedure usually goes much quicker than the original training as you have already taught the dog to do this behaviour on cue, so to do this behaviour on another cue is much easier and quicker to learn. This is also described in practical terms in the next chapter when we change the Target Touch Stick behaviour from a simple 'touch', to a new behaviour called 'spin'.

Of all the basic principles of behaviour, stimulus control and stimulus discrimination is one of the most complex and difficult areas to understand. For more information than this book has described, please see the References page.

Generalisation

Generalisation is an important concept related to stimulus discrimination training. By generalisation we mean the tendency for the effects of training to transfer or spread to other environments. It is essential that all behaviours that the dog learns to perform be trained under all circumstances. The goal of training is stimulus control, which means that a stimulus (cue) triggers a learned behaviour regardless of the setting with a positive outcome.

Generalisation could also be described as teaching the behaviour the dog has learned in the natural settings such as in your home, and then training to spread the effects of training to other environments. You must also train in a manner that promotes stimulus generalisation. This means the dog needs to practice behaviours in different settings, at different times of the day, and in the presence of different people and dogs. So if you have a puppy or dog you would train:

- In your home
- In your garden
- In a friend's home
- In a friend's garden
- Puppy training class
- Road work, quiet road
- In a field with no distractions
- In a field and add one distraction at a time
- In a busy park
- Country walks
- Parade of shops
- Larger shopping centre

The list is endless, but as you educate your dog, each time you go to a new environment go back to 'kindergarten'. If your dog sits for one minute at home, cue for a ten seconds sit, reinforce and build from there. If he heels for twenty paces, walk five paces, reinforce and build from there. If you have trained your dog to 'speak' on cue for twenty seconds, reinforce the dog barking for three seconds and build from there.

Define the target behaviour so as to include many variations. If you want to train many forms of behaviour, then you have to include many different forms of behaviour in your training. Make the training situations resemble natural situations. The greater similarity between the setting in which the behaviour occurs and the setting in which the desired behaviour is to occur, the greater the generalisation.

Observe the target behaviour in natural settings and vary the geographical location of the training, the physical placement, environmental equipment, the dogs and people present, noise, activity levels, indoor and outdoor settings, time of day and other conditions that promote generalisation.

Click!

Practical - Variable reinforcement, Chaining, Generalisation...

Come when called

Coming when called is one of the most basic essential behaviours we need to teach our dogs and can be taught with a simple reverse chain. By the way, most owners make the mistake of trying to teach this behaviour outside, instead of starting in their own home. Many assume that the dog will come readily and consistently when they call him in his familiar environment. Before we start to train our dogs outside, we need to work out what we need to achieve inside our own home.

Step 1. Define target behaviour: 'come when called'. Write a brief description of what you need to teach your dog.

- When the dog is in the same room
- When the dog is in the next room
- When the dog is in the garden
- When the dog is in the same room and a family member present
- When the dog is in the next room and a family member present
- When the dog is in the garden and a family member is present
- When the dog is in the same room and a friendly dog is present
- When the dog is in the next room and a friendly dog is present
- When the dog is in the garden and a friendly dog is present

Add other distractions as you succeed, for example you could add more than one family member. You could add a friend or relation to the

behaviour. We could also teach our dog that when he comes to us he sits and has his collar felt, so that we can put a lead on him without him wanting to disappear.

The first thing that I like to do is teach the dog where he needs to target. We will start by shaping the end behaviour where the dog needs to be sitting in front of the handler who is holding the collar.

With the dog sitting in front of you, take hold of the collar slowly and C/T. Its important that we keep still and quiet while we condition. If the dog moves after the click, that's okay. Repeat this behaviour and gradually speed up your grabbing behaviour, C/T.

Now use the other hand to grab the collar, repeat this exercise as before. The dog is now getting quite used to you holding and grabbing the collar. Another exercise to teach the dog would be to have his collar felt while he is standing in front of you, so that he is nice and calm when having the lead put on. Repeat the behaviour as in the sit. The dog stands in front of you touch his collar, C/T.

Now teach the dog to move slightly to you to have his collar felt. With the dog in front of you (1 foot away), hold your hand out at head height and wait until he moves to you. If he has got the idea he should force his neck and collar in you're hand, C/T. The next step would be to repeat the exercise and when the dog has placed his collar in your hand, withhold the click so that it buys us enough time to put the lead on.

Now we are ready to start 'come when called'.

Begin by having your dog in the same room as you are, and have a clicker and food readily available. Get your dogs attention by calling his name in an excited tone of voice (what's known as care soliciting). Try to resist the temptation to raise your voice. When he looks at you, show him your hand and when he gets to you C/T.

Remember to smile as he approaches you and when he comes within reach, do not grab at his collar, but touch it gently with one hand, C/T. You can repeat this part of exercise several times, depending on how long your dog is able to concentrate. It is better to do one or two 'come when called' ten times a day rather than ten repetitions once a day.

Be unpredictable, do this at odd times of the day. At this stage ALWAYS C/T when you're dog responds. If the dog does not respond, don't give him a second chance. Let him see you put the clicker and treats away and go about your business, totally ignoring him. Its his loss but no big deal to you.

For puppies and timid dogs start 'come when called' with you sitting on the floor. Call him by his name and if he looks at you show him your target hand and wait until he makes some progress towards you, C/T. Get up and move, try again, and then repeat.

We now need to repeat this exercise of 'coming when called' and add a cue: Dogs name-'Come' signal = response = C/T

We have faded out the hand target and replaced it with a verbal cue 'come'. Only use the hand target if the dog gets stuck.

When you are satisfied with his response it is time to improve your dogs performance by starting to put this behaviour on to a variable schedule of reinforcement. By selecting only the fast 'come when called' behaviours and ignoring slow behaviour you keep him guessing as to which behaviour is going to produce the reward he wants.

Step 2. Now we are ready to call the dog from another room. Call him once by using his name and the "come" signal. Wait until he reaches you; touch his collar, C/T

Repeat the instructions as in the same room and when happy with the response change to variable reinforcement, again only select the faster responses.

Step 3. When the dog is in the garden, stand in the house out of site, call the dog once using his name then the "come" signal.

Wait until he reaches you, touch his collar, C/T. Repeat previous instructions using variable reinforcement.

Step 4. If we are happy with the performance so far, raise the criteria by adding a sit, feel the collar, C/T. The sequence goes:

Dogs name = come = sit = feel collar = C/T.

If you have been reinforcing the dog in the sit position in front of you as a separate exercise the dog should have a good idea about the position that you want him to achieve.

Add new criteria?

"Dogs name" = "come" = "sit" = feel collar = put on lead = C/T

Once the behaviour is reliable and solid, repeat previous instructions using variable reinforcement.

Step 5. Go out to a completely safe area free of any distractions, fasten a long line (30ft +) onto you're dogs collar for safety and then remove the dogs lead. Allow him to wander away and when he gets to near the end of the line, put your foot on it and call him. Do not hold on to the line, or pick it up at any stage; it is merely attached for safety's sake, to prevent him from running off.

Call him and when he returns, feel his collar, clip the lead on and C/T. Then remove the lead and repeat exercise several more times varying the distance that you call him, but always before the line becomes tight. When you do the final "come when called" before returning home, make sure it is not carried out in the same spot each time within your training area, so that your dog cannot predict when the lead is about to be put on to go home.

If there are two of you play a game of ping pong, call the dog to each other and C/T for every response, then change the game to every two responses, then every three, be unpredictable. Never show the dog the food or the toy; remember the dog is working for clicks when he gets to the person. That is when the learning takes place, so that the dog learns that I can cause a click and earn a treat. What your dog should learn after a few sessions is to "come when called", to have his collar felt to put his lead on.

He will also learn that having a lead on does not inhibit his freedom in any way.

When you are satisfied with his response you can begin to add in distractions, just as you did at home.

Sometimes, with a dog that has begun coming regularly and consistently he completely looses it! He suddenly has an attack of "selected deafness" to your voice. Call the dog, give the dog an opportunity to succeed and if the behaviour does not happen take the dog straight home, without pausing for sniffs, or us touching or making a fuss. The next time you go out you may see the return to its previous responses. If you have gradually shaped the behaviour step by step it less likely that you will have this problem. As there is no point in giving this cool treatment to your dog until the dog is already performing the desired behaviour freely and at will.

Step 6. Come when called being such important behaviour needs maintenance throughout your dog's life. Use the canine reinforcement analysis you have produced for your dog and use it in every day events to "recall" the dogs quick return to you.

For example you can call him for his dinner, call him for his special game, and call him to give him his favourite bone, click when he gets to you. Make the "come when called" behaviour good news for your dog as one day this practice may save the day.

Practical - Prompting, Stimulus Control...

Targeting

You can use the Target Touch Stick as your prompt to make the dog go where you want, instead of baiting with food, or physical pushing and pulling. You can target the dog onto a grooming table, onto agility equipment, over jumps, or walk in the "heel" position on or off a loose lead. Because the dog offers these behaviours freely and at will, once learned, he will remember and understand them more easily. Using targets such as a target touch stick, your hand, plastic lid or a square piece of card are used just as a means to and end. It is an easy behaviour to teach any age of dog, that by touching your chosen object with his nose he will earn a C/T. To begin teaching targeting you will need your clicker, a target and some treats.

Target Touch Stick.

A Target Touch Stick (TTS) can be a piece of dowel rod, wooden spoon, tracking pole (without the spike), or you can buy a target stick which folds into four for easy carrying from: Crosskeys Select Books. Make sure that the end the dog touches has a contrasting colour. This can easily be accomplished by putting some coloured tape around the end of the stick. The length of the stick depends on the size of your dog and the types of behaviours that you want to teach. I use a fold up version of about 2 feet and have also a 4 feet collapsible version. It is best to start practising holding the stick and clicker in the same hand.

I am right handed so I hold the clicker between my thumb and forefinger of that hand, then place the TTS in between my remaining three fingers. It feels a little bit awkward at first but it is not impossible and allows me to use my left hand to deliver the treat. Now rotate your wrist so that the TTS is pointing straight down, as if you where stirring a pot of porridge.

Our target behaviour is to shape your dog to touch the TTS with his nose. Hold the TTS slightly above the dog's nose and a little to one side, a few inches away. Now keep perfectly still and wait, if he glances at it C/T. Many dogs will naturally investigate new objects and sniff them, so as your dog investigates by sniffing the TTS, or as his nose touches or nearly touches the tip of the TTS, C/T. Make sure you capture this just as it happens.

If your dog totally ignores it, put some peanut butter on the tip, and as your dog goes to sniff/lick it, C/T. The peanut butter serves as a treat. Once your dog's interest in the TTS has increased move the TTS to the other side of your dog's nose and repeat procedure at least five times. When raising criteria, always wait for something more to happen, such as the dog moving a step or two to touch the TTS.

Now move the TTS a little further away and as your dog moves towards it C/T. Have the dog following the TTS from left to right for a C/T. Repeat behaviour from right to left, C/T. Now move the TTS from left to right, back to left for a C/T.

Place the TTS close to the dog again and C/T touches to the left, to the right, above his nose and then to the floor. Settle for small movements and try to make it easy for the dog at first.

When the dog is eagerly touching and following the TTS, Do NOT C/T every touch, C/T only every second, third or fourth touch. Omit reinforcement for touches that are grabs with open mouth or bites, C/T only the behaviour that is on target, faster touches and longer follow throughs. Every shaping session is a unique experience, what you do depends on the response from your dog.

Work on shaping the touch behaviour at least two sessions a day (5 minutes at most) Within a week the dog should understand the concept. It is most important that the dog is able to reliably touch the TTS every time he sees it.

Once this has been achieved you are ready to add the cue word "touch" right before he touches. Repeat shaping procedure using the cue word "touch". Teach "touch" 30 to 50 times until you are getting a reliable response when giving the cue. Then increase the criteria by only reinforcing the better touches and longer follow throughs, using the cue. Remember that to get true reliability we need to teach that in the absence of the cue the behaviour must be extinguished, i.e. only reinforce the behaviour when you have given the cue. Now your dog has mastered this learning you are able to see how useful just this small behaviour could be. If the dog is reliably following your target we have a way of manipulating, or getting the dog to move without even having to touch him.

Practical - Prompting, transferring the stimulus control...

An easy behaviour: SPIN.

When training any behaviour it is always a good idea to visualise the whole behaviour and try and break it down into small pieces. I always think of an orange with all those juicy segments. Just think of shaping, as an orange and train one segment at a time.

Start with the dog standing in front of you. Hold the TTS at nose height (if you hold the TTS at nose level and gently move the TTS just above and behind your dog's head, nice and slowly, he will probably follow the TTS and sit). Move the TTS very slowly to one side (1 segment) and give the cue 'touch'. C/T any head movement in that direction.

Repeat instructions and over time increase the level of movement to (2 segments). Increase very slowly to a / of a spin, C/T, then a fi of the behaviour. C/T. Gradually increasing the behaviour until you have used the TTS to lead your dog into a tight circle, C/T. Once you can establish that the behaviour will occur when you say 'touch' we are then now ready to change the cue, to 'SPIN'.

Changing or adding cues is a fairly simple process. Just remember that

you need to give the NEW cue first then add the old cue. Over time your dog will perform the behaviour on just the new cue alone. So we need to change the cue from 'TOUCH' to 'SPIN'. Remind your dog shaping the behaviour a couple of times with the cue 'touch' = behaviour = C/T. Now we are ready to give the new cue, the sequence goes:

'spin' = 'touch' = behaviour = C/T. Over time you can fade out the 'touch' cue as the dog now performs on the 'spin' cue.

Now teach the reverse spin, you shape the behaviour in the opposite direction. Most dogs have a preferred direction to turn, you may find this a little bit harder for your dog if this is his non-preferred side. How do you test which is the preferred side? Easy just throw a ball 10 times and watch how the dog turns counting the times it happens on each side.

I will leave you to decide on a cue when the behaviour is reliable and consistent

Training notes:

In this process of learning we used continuous reinforcement (no cue), Variable reinforcement (no cue), continuous reinforcement (cue added), variable reinforcement (cue added), continuous reinforcement (new cue, old cue) and variable reinforcement (new cue, old cue faded).

Practical - Generalisation...

Let's go, walk with me.

Learning to follow a Target Touch Stick can teach your dog the desired position for casual walking, heeling or for gaiting in the show ring.

Step 1. Define target behaviour: "Let's go". Write a brief description of what you need to teach your dog. = For example:

- Dog walking on a loose lead = left and right side
- Dog walking off lead = left and right side
- Without distractions
- With distractions added.
- Speed: normal pace, fast pace, slow pace
- Direction: straight line, clockwise circles, anti-clockwise circles, left turn, right turn, start walking, stop walking.
- Locations: home = garden = roads = parks = shopping centre = clicker training club = and much more!

You may decide that you want to teach your puppy to walk close to you on and off the lead on your left-hand side.

Step 1. Start indoors in a room or in the hall where you have enough room to walk around. Show the dog the target touch stick (TTS) give the cue "touch" C/T. This will refresh his memory and at the same time you will see if he is "up for it".

This is a good habit to get into, especially in the early stages of a training programme as it fires up the brain with a tasty treat.

The TTS needs to be at nose level height.

Hold the Target Touch Stick at nose height

on your left side, step forward with your left leg, as soon as the puppy moves with you click, stop and treat. At this stage always stop after a click and feed as eating on the hoof and doing the behaviour at the same time can be confusing to the puppy. Where the puppy gets his treat is irrelevant, what matters is when he got the click, was he beside your left leg? Yes, click! The puppy needs continuous reinforcement to the touch rule even though his feet and the stick are now moving forward. As the puppy behaviour becomes reliable in offering the touch while-walking behaviour, begin to click an instant before the puppy actually touches the TTS.

This is the puppy's early learning of the behaviour of following rather than touching.

Repeat these instructions and if the dog is with you, Click, stop and treat.

Now take three steps before you click, click if the dog is next to you. Now turn around (clockwise) if he follows C/S/T.

Now go back the other way, click every three steps. If your dog is 'up for it' click every four or five steps.

Step 2. Add variations. Speed up a little and if your puppy is still with you, C/S/T. Play a game of "catch up" move around in different directions and as you change direction if your puppy is moving close with you C/S/T. (This game can be played without the Target Touch Stick. The handler starts with the puppy sitting in the heel position on the left and reinforces generously. Move off with your left foot and C/S/T every time the dog is in the 'heel' position.

Move in a large anti-clockwise circle. There are no commands to this game as we need to teach the puppy to stay focused on our movements. The dog needs to work out that the "heel" position is the all-important place where reinforcement occurs. With-out the TTS, handlers should be prepared to keep walking if the puppy stops for a sniff. Eventually the puppy will get back into a reinforcing heel position. A puppy that maintains the "heel" position should get generous reinforcement at first every 3-4 steps, then increase step by step until you have completed a circle. Make the game just hard enough to allow the dog lots of success).

Make it easy for him to win, if he loses concentration and moves off target, do not tell him off! just click when he gets in position. He has already learned to move off with you, now try stopping, and click the puppy for staying close when you stop. Always make sure that TTS is at nose level when you are moving around, later when the behaviour is fluent we can fade the TTS so that the puppy just targets you!

Keep sessions short on a 'little and often' basis and make sure that when you click the puppy's behaviour is on target. Before moving the training programme outside introduce the lead and repeat previous instructions, step by step.

Step 3. Move to the garden and repeat 'step one' making sure there are no distractions of any kind. Also make sure that you begin at the beginning as every time we change location we need to go back to "kindergarten" and refresh the puppy's memory as to what he is supposed to be doing. As this is a secure environment your puppy can stay off lead. Repeat step 2, make a nice game of it. Add the lead and repeat previous instructions, especially the go back to "kindergarten" rule.

Step 4. Now you are ready for the big world outside, lead attached to the puppy for safety's sake. You can put the loop of the lead over your wrist and tuck your arm in tight to your body, or you can tie the lead to your waist so that you are not tempted to jerk the puppy on the lead. I recommend a double training lead to my students which goes over the shoulder, freeing both hands, one to hold the TTS and a clicker and one to deliverer the treat. Start again at the very beginning; step off with your left foot, if puppy follows, C/S/T. go through steps 1,2,3, as before any pulling on the lead go back to 'kindergarten'. Keep sessions 'short and sweet'.

Socialisation and habituation must be undertaken as early as possible to desensitise our best friend.

Training notes: As your puppy moves with you, his eyes should be focused on the TTS as though he is going to touch it.

If your puppy is not looking at the TTS, stop and wait for the dog to look at the TTS, click the instant the puppy looks at it. Remember to follow each click with a treat. When the puppy fully understands the TTS is to be followed in a certain position you can start to fade the TTS and add a verbal cue/command.

Clicking the puppy for being in the same position as he was while following the TTS, will convey to the puppy that it is his position that is be reinforced.

Practical

Go Out / Send Away

This behaviour is essential to training a dog in agility, flyball, working trials, obedience and field trials. A solid 'go out' for competition or for just having some fun with your dog is a great behaviour to teach. For the 'go out' you need a clicker, some food reinforcer and a target. The target I use for this exercise is a tracking pole with a point to stick in the ground, but a garden cane or a piece of doweling is equally suitable.

Repeat previous exercises with this new target so that the dog touches it freely and at will, my Emma is fixated by it!

Give the cue "touch" and if you have been doing your homework the dog should immediately touch it with his nose. Repeat this behaviour three or four times or until the dog consistently touches the target. Next stick the target into the ground and move one pace away from the target. Give the cue "touch" wait a moment to see if the dog touches the target and if he does C/T. If he doesn't touch the target pull the target out of the ground and offer the target and get several good responses before trying again. Replace the target in the ground and get several successful touches. Once the dog is moving towards the target now is the time to add some distance. If you are watching your dog carefully you will notice a pattern developing.

- The dog is looking at you.
- You say "touch".
- The dog turns and moves away to touch the target.
- You click just at the moment the dog touches the target.
- The dog comes back to your location.
- You offer a treat.
- You repeat the exercise

The easiest way to increase the distance that your dog needs to travel is to take a step backwards from the target. On each repetition, after you say "touch", your dog will turn and travel to the target. While the dog is moving towards the target, take a step backward. Over a cycle of repetitions, your distance to the target will gradually increase. Please make small steps; so as to allow your dog to get used to the idea of moving away from you. The trainer's goal is to get between a three metre and ten metres 'go out' within a couple of sessions depending on the age, size and temperament of the dog. Increase the distance carefully until you can get a couple of good 'go outs' in a row of at least ten metres away from the target.

Now that you have something to work with it is time to tidy up the behaviour. Every beginning dog that I have seen doing this exercise will have 'go outs' that are variable! Some just don't quite touch the target and some arc to get to the target.

If you want precision in your training (straight send aways) send your dog to the target by using the "touch" cue and if you see any hesitation or deviation call your dog back to you the instant the dog makes an error and start again. You can also reduce the distance that you send the dog and reinforce straight send away behaviour, you are now laying a foundation for straight send aways over a longer distance. Remember to work in a quiet and safe outdoor area without the lead.

Recalling your dog at the moment he makes a mistake terminates the target behaviour and allows you to carry on.

At this stage of the training you should be able to get your dog to a target at least to a distance of ten metres.

When you are ready to transfer the cue to your "away" signal, it goes like this. Give new verbal signal = "away" followed by the "touch" signal. The dog gives response C/T. For the next 30 to 50 repetitions gradually over time fade the "touch" cue so that the dog works to the "away" cue only. With this task-completed start to use a variable ratio reinforcement schedule, very gently, ask for two send aways; (stretch the ratio) gradually increasing the workload.

At this stage of the training you are ready to fade the target. Use the same location; send the dog "away" without the target, reinforce every behaviour. The dog should keep going until he hears the click. This is how you are going to stop the behaviour for a redirection. Vary the distance that the dog performs, sometimes its 10 metres, sometimes 8 metres, sometimes 9 metres and so on.

To teach the stop signal, give the cue "stop" then C/T. The dog will associate the stop signal with the click, which ends the behaviour. You now have foundation behaviour for agility, working trials, obedience and for having some fun.

Schedules of Reinforcement

To teach a dog a new behaviour, or to fine-tune an existing previously learned behaviour or maintain a behaviour, you must know when and how to use reinforcement effectively.

We now need to talk about what behaviourists call schedules of reinforcement. Put another way these are rules governing the delivery of reinforcement. Which responses will be reinforced, and how often.

Reinforcers can be given for every correct response or for only some correct responses. When behaviour is reinforced every time it occurs, this is called continuous reinforcement. When first training a puppy to sit and you click & treat for every correct sit, the puppy is on a continuous reinforcement schedule. Continuous reinforcement is an excellent procedure to use when teaching a new behaviour, but it should gradually be faded to a more functional schedule.

The long term goal of training is to make the dog independent of contrived reinforcers, so that an intermittent reinforcement schedule will be enough to maintain the behaviour, but not enough to make the behaviour dependent on the reinforcer. An experienced dog will work for a good dog signal and a pat on the head.

Intermittent reinforcement schedules can appear pretty perplexing when first approaching this subject.

There are six: Fixed ratio, variable ratio, fixed interval, variable interval, fixed duration and variable duration. This book covers the first two, for further reading see the bibliography page.

A fixed ratio schedule will provide a reinforcer after the target behaviour has occurred n number of times. In fixed ratio or FR schedules the target behaviour must occur a certain number of times before it is reinforced. If the behaviour is FR-1 schedule, the ratio of the number of occurrences of the behaviour is 1-1. In other words, a reinforcer is delivered each and every time the target behaviour occurs. This FR-1 schedule is, of course, the same as continuous reinforcement and so is sometimes abbreviated CRF.

An intermittent FR schedule requires that the target behaviour occurs at a fixed number of times before it is reinforced. If behaviour is on a fixed ratio 3 (FR-3) schedule, for instance, the behaviour has to occur three times before it is reinforced. If it is a FR-10 schedule, it has to occur 10 times before reinforcement. Fixed ratio schedules are easy to use and remember when to deliver the reinforcement because the reinforcement is on a fixed schedule per number of behaviours. The drawback with this schedule is that because the FR schedule is predictable, dogs learn when reinforcement is coming and may hesitate immediately after the reinforcer is given before engaging in the next behaviour.

A variable ratio schedule would provide a reinforcer after the target behaviour has occurred a number of times, with the number varying around an average of n. In variable ratio schedules, reinforcement is delivered after a certain number of responses that vary unpredictably. You are probably aware of some well known variable ratio schedules, such as playing a slot machine, fishing, and having a dabble on the lottery. Variable ratio schedules can also be abbreviated.

In VR-6 schedule, the number of responses required before reinforcement is given varies, but the average number of responses is six. For example the behaviour might be reinforced after occurring four times, seven times, nine times, two times, four times and so on, but on average the ratio of occurrences to reinforcements will be 6/1.

Thanks to the unpredictability of the reinforcers, VR schedules have the power to generate more consistent and rapid responding so that the animal performs at a much higher rate. VR schedules are more resistant to extinction and the animal will work harder and for a longer period of time with very infrequent reinforcement than with other reinforcement schedules.

One drawback is that for beginning trainers, if the VR schedule is set too high in attempting to randomise reinforcement, they may find it hard to use, as this procedure can cause the dog to abruptly quit. This phenomenon is known as ratio strain. By switching abruptly from continuous reinforcement schedule to a high rate VR schedule you are likely to get the same sort of effects you see with extinction.

The frequency of behaviour will fall off and you may get some emotional behaviour, such as aggression or temper tantrums. To prevent ratio strain, you need to avoid abrupt increases in the ratio, Instead you should gradually increase the requirement for reinforcement by stretching the ratio.

Stretching the ratio means gradually increasing the number of times behaviour must be performed to qualify for reinforcement. For example you might want to shape a target behaviour called 'sit' ten times. The target behaviour is not one 'sit' but ten 'sits'. However start by shaping one sit (C/T), when the behaviour is solid and reliable, shape two sits(C/T). When that behaviour is solid and reliable, shape three sits(C/T). When that behaviour is solid and reliable, shape four sits(C/T) and so on. This procedure is called stretching the ratio and is also a form of shaping.

You shape the number of times the behaviour is performed, for each reinforcement. This procedure allows you to obtain more behaviour for the same amount of reinforcement, so long as you stretch the behaviour slowly, or the performance will break down. Over time and effort the dog learns to sit ten times for one reinforcement, has the job finished?.....NO!

Maintenance training is necessary; the job is never complete if we want to have the same high rate of behaviour. Unfortunately a lot of people spend a lot of time reinforcing the desired changes in their dogs behaviour then they stop reinforcing the behaviour, or they reinforce the behaviour so infrequently that the schedule isn't rich enough to maintain behaviour. With Emma my fourteen-year-old dog, we still have fun; learning new tricks and maintaining some of the old behaviour that she could perform in her younger days. Physically she is less active but she still enjoys the mental stimulation that is required to problem solve learning any new behaviour.

Practical

Down stay (with distractions) -
Generalisation, Stimulus Discrimination...

Remember free shaping the 'down' behaviour in a previous chapter? Well once the dog is performing a reliable down, why stop there? For your dog to lay there longer just withhold the click and you also teach him to stay. Increase the time he is lying down by counting to yourself 5 seconds, 10 seconds, 15 seconds, and so on, clicking at the end of each interval with a treat.

Now to introduce some distractions. If you have been seated during this time, stand up when your dog is laying down, if your dog moves sit down and totally ignore until your dog is laying down again. Try standing up and if your dog stays laying down click and treat. He is then allowed to move as the click tells him that the behaviour is over. Wait until your dog lays down again and then you stand up for a count of 5 seconds, if he stays in the down, click and treat. Repeat this behaviour until he is laying for about 30 seconds, enough time for you to reach the door to the room.

You are standing, now take a short step towards the door, you have guessed if he moves go back to sitting. When he lays down, stand up slowly, move a pace towards the door, if he stays in the down position click and throw the treat to him in that position so that he is less likely to move. The dog hasn't moved so you move another step towards the door, and surprise, surprise our dog must be getting the idea of the game, he didn't move. You should be able to shape your behaviour to the door, without your dog moving.

When you get there, just gently tap the door, any movement by the dog start again. If no movement from your dog, click and hand your dog a treat in that position. Move to the door, slightly open it, no response from the dog, close the door, click and go back to your dog and treat in position. Leave your dog, open the door fully, no response from your dog, close the door and repeat previous instructions.

Now leave your dog in position, go to the door open it, go outside, close door, count to 5 open and close door if dog still in position, click and give what you have left and then proceed to have a game that your dog really enjoys. If your dog moved at any stage, just go back to "kindergarten" and start where you and the dog were winning. What you have just taught your dog in a short time is "down stay" with you moving and then you out of sight.

You can teach this to any age of dog, but bear in mind that you do not want to exceed 5 minutes of training at any one session, especially with a puppy or dog who is at the beginning of their education. Once you have completed that task you can start to ask just a little bit more by adding another distraction i.e. another person entering the room.

The dog gets up, the person entering the room has been primed to disappear closing the door behind them before the dog could get that lovely attention. This set-up should be repeated just once more to see if the dog has learnt anything, such as to get the attention from a guest he must keep still.

If the guest enters (one pace into the room) and the dog stays still, click and the guest treats the dog with food in the hand held at the dog's nose level (we must not encourage the dog to jump up). Repeat this behaviour by allowing the guest to move nearer and nearer to the dog before we click and treat. With this success you can now add another distraction, such as the guest and a child entering the room. Please feel free to add distractions as you go one at a time until you have three people as distraction and then four, a whole family and so on. At this point we haven't added the cue or command to the equation. But if you would like to, just give the signal just as the behaviour happens.

By withholding the click the dog also learns to stay at the same time, so that when you say "down" the dog will stay there until you click or you use a release word such as "okay".

For this procedure wait until the dog goes to lay down and give the cue "down" just as it is about to happen, then click and throw the food slightly short of where the dog is laying so that he has to get up and get it! If he comes looking for more food, as usual totally ignore him and you will be amazed to watch that he will go and lay down, just as he does, repeat procedure. When giving the cue just before the behaviour happens, it may cause the dog to slow down. This is a natural occurrence as he is now learning that this sound is the trigger for that behaviour, and your dog's reaction time can be speeded up later.

So far we have been using continuous reinforcement, at this stage we need to introduce variable reinforcement so that we build in the reliability to his performance. So we have a behaviour called "down" which needs to be speeded up so we need to discriminate against the slow downs so that the dog learns, when we say down we get a fast response. We give the cue, get the response and decide was it of the right quality, if it was he gets a click and treat, if not, we try again.

Once the dog is performing a "fast" "down", why not take this behaviour a step forward! Train your dog to respond to the door bell with a down behaviour, this sounds complex but if you have achieved fast downs on "cue" with distractions then all it requires is transferring the cue.

Present the new stimulus (doorbell) give old cue "Down" wait for response, C/T. Use continuous reinforcement and when happy with the response, increase the performance as before by only C/T quick downs (variable reinforcement).

Have a friend help with the doorbell or if you are proficient with electrical appliances set a bell push inside the house so that you are then in full control of the new stimulus. Once you have conditioned the dog with the new stimulus (doorbell), fade the "down" cue from the instructions given to the dog. In other words just ring the bell, once, and when he downs, C/T. If no response, go back a step, try again with a bell ring, give down cue and C/T for down behaviour. Repeat a couple of times and then just ring the bell and C/T for the down behaviour.

So far we have been C/T for fast downs, we now need to add another criteria, stay, so by withholding the click we get a longer performance, we need to shape a "long down" of at least a couple of minutes.

The procedure should read: Doorbell = Down Behaviour = Delayed Click (start from 1 second to 2minutes very slowly). Now you are ready to invite a friend round for a coffee. Your friend arrives ringing the doorbell the dog responds with a down you leave the room and close the door and then proceed to answer the front door and invite your friend in. Enter the room where the dog is laying and if still in the same position, both enter and sit down, then click and your friend treats.

Extinction - eliminate the negative!

In previous chapters we have talked about behaviour characteristics being classified into two categories: One is where a behaviour doesn't occur often enough; the other is where a behaviour occurs too often. So far we have concentrated on the first kind of behaviour, and the procedure for increasing behaviour - reinforcement. Where a behaviour occurs too often we must look at ways of reducing the behaviour. One way of doing this is called extinction.

A small sample of dog behaviours comes to mind: such as mugging your house guest, begging at the table, whining while in a crate, stealing your Sunday lunch, barking at the window and much more.

Okay, so there are lots of problems when behaviour occurs too often. With these problems the task is not to strengthen the target behaviour but to weaken it, to get it to occur less frequently.

We have described how operant behaviour is maintained by its consequences. We have seen it working in the case of reinforcement. Thinking about our A>B>C equation then it follows that preventing these consequences that maintain behaviour should weaken it. We need to think about what is reinforcing the behaviour already. It has to be the case that if a behaviour happens with embarrassing frequency (that we could bet money on), there must be a 'pay off'.

If we can arrange the environment so that the behaviour no longer pays off, then it will occur less often - that's extinction. Extinction refers to the extinction not of an animal (a drastic solution) but of a behaviour, a behaviour that dies down by itself for lack of reinforcement.

Just think of a dead battery, the battery is still there but has not been charged up! In extinction, the dog may remain quite capable of performing the undesirable behaviour but does not do so.

For example, Ben the Jack Russell puppy is put into a 'play pen' to give his owner a break to do other things. A few minutes later Ben barks at the owner, who then smiles and talks in a sweet way to console him (unintentional reinforcement). This goes on for a couple of weeks. The frequency of barking increases and Ben's owner makes a determined effort not to pay him any attention at all, including, letting him out of the pen, telling him off, talk to him, looking at him if he barks and whines. The barking drops off. That does not mean however that your puppy has forgotten how to bark, only that the rate of barking has declined. So after a few minutes of quiet behaviour you may decide to let him out for a game or to see if he wants to go to the toilet.

So extinction does not mean that the behaviour is 'extinct'. You may have heard of behaviour that has been extinguished. This means that the behaviour has been reduced by the extinction procedure. The effect of extinction is to reduce the frequency of the target behaviour. Extinction is a simple procedure: prevent the target behaviour from being reinforced and it declines, but as with reinforcement, extinction is more difficult to implement than it appears.

We need to be particularly careful when using extinction to follow the guidelines. We can follow similar rules to using reinforcement but pay particular attention to the warnings.

1. Define the target behaviour.

Defining the behaviour you want to change is just as important when it comes to decreasing the rate of behaviour as it is when you want to increase the rate of behaviour. Any time you are attempting to change the frequency of a behaviour you must have a clear idea of what that behaviour is. If you have a dog with a list of problem behaviours, it is prudent to work on the problem behaviour on top of your list. One at a time! Not all problem behaviours should be treated with extinction. You should never ignore behaviours that are potentially dangerous or that are harmful to the dog, animal or any person.

2. Identify the reinforcers that maintain the target behaviour.

If operant behaviour happens with regularity you can safely assume that it is being reinforced. To put the behaviour on extinction you have to identify the reinforcers. To determine what reinforcer is maintaining the target behaviour you will need to observe the behaviour and its consequences. There is a good chance that the consequences are reinforcing the behaviour. For instance every time Ben the puppy barked in the 'play pen' the owner paid attention to him, so it was reasonable to suppose that barking was being reinforced by human attention. Behaviour can have all sorts of consequences, and identifying those that are reinforcing a particular behaviour is sometimes difficult. Change the environment for the dog and barking takes on another meaning. The dog that barks looking out the front window, or barks when the postman starts to walk up the path, it is not your behaviour that is reinforcing but the people passing in the street.

3. Withhold all reinforcement of the target behaviour.

Withholding all reinforcement of the target behaviour is not easy, but assuming that you have identified the relevant reinforcers, you are in with a chance. In the case of the dog that barks at the window at passing strangers in the street, one option is to prevent the consequences that work on the dog by arranging the environment. Move the dog from the window into another room away from the front of the house. Consider Ben that barks while in the 'play pen'. Withholding reinforcers required only the co-operation of the owner but had the whole family paid attention to the barking, the difficulty of reducing the problem behaviour could have been increased.

Imagine if the reinforcement was on a variable ratio (partial) schedule so that only some of the time barking was reinforced, when it was really irritating and other times the behaviour was ignored.

When Alex the Labrador begs at the table for food he doesn't always get what he wants all the time, just the occasional food tit bit thrown to the dog. This could have the effect of maintaining the behaviour at very high rates and may even make the behaviour more difficult to eliminate.

This phenomenon is known as the partial reinforcement effect and refers to the effect of increased resistance to extinction following intermittent reinforcement. Resistance to extinction varies directly with the frequency of reinforcement. In other words, the more often behaviour is reinforced, the more resistant to extinction. This runs counter to PRE. It is clear that behaviour can be maintained by occasional reinforcement. With this information we could look at the problem behaviour with this information to hand. The reinforcement schedule that is in place before extinction will determine if the behaviour will decrease quickly or if there will be a more gradual decrease. When extinction follows continuous reinforcement, the behaviour may decrease more rapidly. When extinction follows partial (variable ratio) reinforcement, extinction is more gradual. In conclusion does this mean that we should reinforce unwanted behaviour continuously for a time before putting it on extinction? Some behaviourists have suggested as much. Extinction can be used as an alternative to more intensive procedures like punishment, for some behaviours.

4.   Observe the results.

As with reinforcement, it is essential that you observe behaviour during extinction. To be certain that the extinction procedure is working is to note changes in behaviour during extinction. If you do not see typical extinction effects, the chances are the consequence you are withholding is not the relevant reinforcer.

Problems with extinction........out of control reinforcement!

What could be a simple procedure of withholding reinforcement to the target behaviour can turn out to be a very different story. The problem is that the target behaviour may produce reinforcement from a variety of sources and those sources are often difficult to control. Often members of the family, friends, neighbours and other people tend to inadvertently reinforce behaviours that you are trying extinguish.

Some dogs leap about, jump up, mouth and nudge people in greeting because they have not been educated, in fact they have been reinforced for it by hand contact on the head, waving hands about, excitable high pitched voices and other kinds of attention. Watch puppies jumping up, striving for eye contact and trying to get their owner's attention, and of course when they get fifty pounds heavier and it is a wet and muddy day, you soon see a change in communication!

Another source of reinforcement that is difficult to control are behaviours that are self-reinforcing.

Nobody has to pat me on the back to keep me drinking my favourite claret, I drink it because I enjoy it.

The puppy that chews on furniture and inappropriate items doesn't do it because somebody does something reinforcing. For puppies, chewing on stuff is just reinforcing in itself.

Young dogs and puppies provide a good example. They have lots of energy to burn. It may be that running around the house occurs (that mad half hour people often talk about), not because someone is providing reinforcing consequences for that behaviour, but because it feels good to run around.

The point to make at this juncture is that if target behaviour is going to be reinforced, either because someone is not co-operating with the intervention effort or because the behaviour is self-reinforcing, then extinction is probably not going to work.

Extinction Bursts: The lull after the storm

Extinction produces some rather startling side effects. The long-term effect on behaviours that are no longer reinforced will be a steady and pronounced reduction in the frequency of the target behaviour, and it may eventually completely stop!

But before the behaviour stops the immediate effect of putting behaviour on extinction will be a sudden and rapid increase in the target behaviour. This is an extinction burst. A sharp increase in the frequency, duration or intensity of the behaviour on extinction. Such bursts can be seen when extinction is used to reduce the frequency of the dog that begs. In begging, reinforcement is on a variable ratio schedule-the one most resistant to extinction.

In the case of Alex the Labrador, begging was reinforced with the occasional tit bits from the table.

When the owner decided to stop reinforcing the behaviour, Alex who would normally sit without being asked, like a good boy, became quite highly charged. Alex's behaviour change was sudden and rapid. Alex whined, which quickly led to barking. He paced from person to person at the table, he then reached up with a paw and scratched his owner on the leg, he then tried to jump up onto the table to take it for himself! Alex's behaviour increased in frequency and intensity and was the classic extinction burst. His owners persevered, however, and Alex did eventually stop begging. The extinction burst may be the cause for some people trying to use extinction eventually to give up and give in. If you do provide reinforcement during extinction burst, you are likely to reinforce at a higher rate of behaviour or more intense levels of the target behaviour.

Another side effect of extinction of the target behaviour is an increase in the variability of the behaviour. In the case of Alex the Labrador the behaviour of begging usually produces a pay-off (partial reinforcement) then if it doesn't work, you see all kinds of variation in the behaviour. Not only did he become highly charged but elicited an emotional outburst. Emotional behaviours such as aggression, rage or complete frustration may appear during extinction bursts. So if you are going to use extinction to deal with problem behaviour you have to let everyone involved know that the problem behaviour may get worse before it gets better.

Spontaneous Recovery, where did that come from!

Sometimes after the successful completion of the extinction procedure, when the target behaviour is said to be extinguished, the behaviour suddenly reappears. When this happens, it is called spontaneous recovery. The reappearance of the target behaviour following its extinction.

For Alex the Labrador that begged at the table, begging stopped when extinction was used. But once in a while even though no reinforcement was provided, Alex would approach the table and start begging. Spontaneous recovery need not be a problem so long as the behaviour is not reinforced when it recovers, but unfortunately, if just one family member gives in and reinforces Alex with food during spontaneous recovery the effects of extinction would be completely undone.

If that happens the extinction procedure must be repeated, the good news is, as extinction has taken place it will take far less time the second time around.

Understanding extinction has many benefits for decreasing and increasing behaviours. In training, to keep behaviours from extinction, you need to eventually get to the point where you are using intermittent reinforcement. For an experienced trainer using extinction bursts enables you to move more rapidly toward your target behaviour. A skilled shaper may even omit reinforcers (clicks) specifically in order to provoke a sharp increase in the frequency, duration or intensity of the behaviour. Dog behaviourist Gary Wilkes calls this surfing the extinction bursts.

Differential Reinforcement

Increasing the desirable, decreasing the undesirable!

As can be seen, there are some problems using extinction. Fortunately most of these problems can be avoided when extinction is used in combination with reinforcement, so simply ignoring undesirable behaviour is not sufficient.

Differential reinforcement is any procedure that combines extinction and reinforcement to change the frequency of a target behaviour. So if we want behaviour to occur less often, we could provide reinforcement when the behaviour occurs at a lower rate DRL - the procedure of reinforcing the target behaviour only when it occurs at a low rate.

Differential reinforcement of low rate can be use to reduce barking. One of the dog sections for a local council had a dog that barked while in transit from park to park.

The average trip lasted fifteen minutes in which this dog barked all the way. As these security dog handlers had been educated to clicker training on a one-week course at "Crosskeys" they learned the principles of operant conditioning. It wasn't long before they had worked out a way to reduce the barking to a 'muffled grunt'. The dog handler had worked out what was operating on the dog by eliminating any stimulus that might trigger the barking.

He turned the radio off, he and the dog got into the van and just sat there without the engine on or moving off. By reducing the strength of the stimuli he was able to reinforce quieter barking until he got the 'muffled grunt'. He then added a new stimulus by putting the radio on, barking slightly increased in frequency, again he reinforced lower rate barking to a 'muffled grunt'.

Another new stimulus was added, the engine turned on, slight increase in barking, again he reinforced lower rate of barking until 'muffled grunt' achieved.   At this stage to drive safely we used another handler to reinforce the dog while in transit. The dog was now starting to generalise what was wanted, low frequency barking and when the van moved off we where pleasantly surprised at the response by the dog.

The rate of barking was certainly lower and within a couple of minutes of reinforcing lower rate barking we had the "muffled grunt" once again. The dog handler concerned has now got a dog that barks 'on cue' and is quiet 'off cue' even in transit!

On our training courses I asked the class to reinforce any behaviour that they would like to decrease. One student proceeded to C/T every lower rate behaviour regardless of what behaviour she got. After a couple of minutes of shaping she asked me to come over and watch what she had achieved. The dog was a turbo charged Labrador, which had suddenly learnt to move about in slow motion. So if you want to decrease a behaviour DRL is used when some level of behaviour is acceptable, but less is better.

We can also use differential reinforcement of incompatible behaviour to decrease unwanted behaviour. Indicated by DRI the procedure works by reinforcing a behaviour that is incompatible with the target behaviour. In other words, if a dog is doing one thing, it can't do the other.

A common complaint by pet dog owners is that their dog jumps up on friends and neighbours in their home. A good example of incompatible behaviour would be reinforcing the dog for laying down. If the dog is laying down he cannot be jumping up or greeting in an unsociable way. Another problem with dogs that jump up at home is that they probably do the same thing on the street to strangers.

An alternative incompatible behaviour for jumping up would be sitting. A good behaviour to teach for street work, so the undesirable behaviour decreases and most importantly the dog has acquired a new skill that is an acceptable way of greeting people.

We could also look at DRA which stands for the procedure of reinforcing an alternative behaviour instead of the target behaviour. The idea is you put the target behaviour on extinction and reinforce some alternative behaviour. With DRI we found an incompatible behaviour for jumping up, but it is not always practical to come up with an incompatible behaviour so this is where DRA comes in. DRA gives the animal an alternative way of obtaining reinforcers.

For example Harry the turbo charged dog that barks when the telephone rings. The dog might be given a chance of learning an alternative behaviour such as playing with a 'Buster Cube', withhold some of the dog's favourite kibble and place it in the buster cube ready for use.

Step 1.First of all you need to know that the dog is happy playing with the buster cube

Step 2. Arrange for a friend to telephone you at a particular time (just before the dog's dinnertime), have the buster cube loaded with food and at the ready.

Step 3. When the telephone rings and before the dog starts barking give Harry the buster cube. In this case, the timing of the buster cube reinforcer is crucial so that Harry does not get reinforced when he is barking.

Although these alternative behaviours may not be incompatible with the undesirable behaviour they at least allow Harry to obtain reinforcers for behaviours, which are of the desired target behaviour, less barking is better.

Rules for using Differential Reinforcement.

1. Define the target behaviours.

With differential reinforcement there are normally two target behaviours. You are trying to reduce the frequency of one behaviour while increasing the frequency of another.

We are trying to reduce jumping up and increase the sit and down behaviours. We are trying to reduce barking behaviour to an exceptional level. In some cases the two target behaviours are different rates of the same activity.

2. Put the undesirable target behaviour (or rate) on extinction.

To put the undesirable target behaviour on extinction you need to identify the reinforcers that maintain the problem behaviour. The next step is to then prevent those reinforcers from following the unwanted behaviour. If you are going to use DRA or DRI, you withhold reinforcement of the problem behaviour. If you want to use DRL, you withhold reinforcement of the problem rate of the target behaviour.

While the undesirable behaviour is on extinction, which means the reinforcer must be withheld after every instance of the problem behaviour, you must reinforce the desirable behaviour.

3. Reinforce the desirable target behaviour (or rate).

In a lot of cases the behaviour is not necessarily undesirable but at a too high rate. Barking is quite acceptable if it is at a certain rate but becomes problem behaviour if we have excess.

4. Observe the results.

Differential reinforcement is like a game of chess, once you have implemented the intervention you have to have patience and watch every move that your dog makes, making sure not to allow uncontrolled reinforcement from outside sources.

As an afterthought, be sure that you can handle the responses that may come through extinction, such as aggression, the dog that really becomes very pushy for attention, emotional outbursts and frustration. If not, perhaps a chat with your local APDT member can put your fears at rest. The address and telephone number is available in the resources page.

Conditioned Aversive Stimuli

Avoidance conditioning; a warning signal.

In the canine reinforcement analysis we looked at all the things that the dog liked and would work for. On the other side to positive events we have negative events. Things the dog will avoid and escape from. We could list these negative events and pair them with a new special signal. A timely conditioned positive reinforcer tells the dog, "that we liked that version of the behaviour and here is something for your trouble, so do it some more".

You can also establish a conditioned aversive stimulus, which communicates " I don't like that version of your behaviour, it is not good and something you don't like will happen unless you stop". Using positive reinforcement as your main teaching tool does not mean that you cannot use a "NO" signal when you need to. If the dog is doing something that is not safe to do, a timely "stop that" signal is what we need.

In avoidance conditioning, if behaviour can prevent a negative stimulus from occurring, the behaviour increases in frequency. In order for this to happen the dog must learn that the negative stimulus is coming and must know what he can do to avoid the negative stimulus. This procedure requires conditioning, just like click (positive) means something nice is coming, a new (negative) sound means something you wish to avoid is coming.

The late John Fisher's Dog Training Discs have become very popular around the world, as the use of these brass discs makes a sound which is unique to the dog and one that has been conditioned with the removal of something desirable, in this case, food!

Any new stimulus (sound) can be used to condition the dog that something desirable will be taken away.

Non-Reinforcement Signal.

There has been a great debate about using a non-reinforcement marker signal. It has become popular among dog trainers. The use of words, such as "wrong", "oops", "try again" "too bad" are often spoken in a neutral tone. The idea is that we can give the dog some extra information, by using a signal that signifies, "that will not be reinforced". B.F.Skinner's definition of punishment - taking away something-desirable

-means the "wrong" signal is a conditioned punisher, since it means that reinforcers are not available. For experienced trainers who have a dog with a vast repertoire of fully shaped behaviours and cues, a dog that keeps throwing variable behaviour at you establishing a "wrong" signal could be a useful tool. They can condition the dog to understand the sound as meaning simply "stop what you are doing as you are going down a path that leads to a dead end".

Or put another way, "no reinforcement is available for that version of the behaviour". When giving this "wrong" signal it has to be communicated to the dog "immediately and with certainty" when the undesirable behaviour occurs. Any delay will punish the wrong behaviour.

Punishment, the debate goes on

When the dog is in a situation in which reinforcers are readily available and he performs the undesirable target behaviour, you remove the dog from that reinforcing situation. The dog should not be put in a time out for a long time. Usually several minutes is most effective. When dogs are given a time out and there is no supervision they should be put into a safe, secure area such as a crate. Or put into an environment where no harm can be done to the dog or the surroundings.

This is known as a 'time out' and is used to reduce the frequency of target behaviour by removing the dog from a reinforcing situation. Time out, when used effectively, can be a punisher. If the crate is over used for time outs the crate itself will become a punisher. If this happens the crate will not be a safe, secure den for your dog. For the time out to be effective, the original environment must be more reinforcing than the time out environment.

I suppose the crux of the matter is to know what is a reinforcing environment and what is punishing environment. The definition for punishment is the procedure of providing consequences for a behaviour that decreases the frequency of that behaviour. If a dog likes lots of attention, time outs are likely to succeed. If your dog likes lot of rest and sleep, then time out may not be an effective punisher.

Using punishment does not teach the dog what is safe to do, it only teaches the dog what not to do. One side effect of punishment is that it produces undesirable emotional reactions, particularly fear and anger. Fear may take the form of efforts to escape or avoid anything associated with the punishment. This is undesirable, since escaping or avoiding an aversive event is going to be negatively reinforced!

Murray Sidman PhD., a behaviour analyst who is an expert on punishment- and one of its severest critics, likes to say that people who use shocks become shocks. You become a conditioned punisher because you are paired with the punisher, and if your dog cannot get away from you he may attack you. Even small puppies can paw, bite and struggle with the owner as he attempts to punish, and if the owner backs off, the owner is very likely to reinforce this aggressive behaviour.

You must also be aware that using anything as a conditioned punisher may easily have other consequences. I heard a story recently that a six-year-old dog had bitten a city gent on the thigh while being walked down the street. The dog suddenly attacked for no good reason. It was later said that the dog had apparently attacked unprovoked! This dog had never shown any signs of aggression and after a health check was found to be quite a friendly dog. On further investigation the man in the suit was holding a rolled up newspaper and was hailing a cab by the side of the road. This dog's early learning included being threatened with a rolled up newspaper.

So if you use punishment you may find that there are toxic side effects, as you cannot expect those animals whose behaviour you punish to be glad to see you coming, particularly if you use some form of physical punishment.

Shaping, the training game

The training game is a great way to sharpen your shaping skills and have fun at the same time. First described in Karen Pryor's Don't Shoot the Dog (a definite must read, see resources page). It allows you to see and experience other trainers decision points, and to be aware of what you might have done instead. It allows trainers to make mistakes and learn from them without confusing some poor dog or unsuspecting person! Playing the game demonstrates the importance of accurate timing. It also gives people an idea of how the animal feels during the shaping process.

To play the training game you need at least two people, a trainer and a subject. You will also need a clicker and some primary reinforcers (sweets!). In my Clicker Workshops I often demonstrate the game by being the trainer and asking a volunteer subject to be the 'dog'.

After that I would get pairs of volunteers to play both roles. We have the subject leave the room and the students decide on the behaviour to be shaped. The behaviour must be something easy to do physically which everyone can see. Some favourites are turning in a circle, standing on a particular square looking in a certain direction, standing still and clapping hands, pouring or drinking water, or turning on a light switch.

For more experienced students we go for two or three step behaviours such as: picking up an object and perhaps giving it to someone, making a cup of tea, walking and clapping hands, go to a chair pick it up move to a target area and sit on it. Some of the students have become quite creative, but all the behaviours are sociably acceptable and safe to do! Before the game begins it is essential that the students understand the importance of reinforcing the smallest approximations, although until they actually do it for themselves they are inclined to wait until they have the whole behaviour before the reinforcing. You could wait forever!

The student subject is brought into the room and instructed to begin moving randomly around the room and listen for clicks. Each time the student subject hears the click, he or she must return to the trainer and get an imaginary treat. This prevents the student subject from just standing in one spot and trying to think, which gives you nothing to reinforce. The student subject will also need to remember what he or she was doing when they where clicked.

After playing in hundreds of training games we seem to get the same responses from the student subjects, they get fixated with the trainer; they watch for any sign or signal, in particular any facial or body movements, which might help them with the puzzle (this happens with dogs as well as people and if you continually have food on your person this adds to the fixation on the trainer instead of the behaviour being shaped). Some get stuck at the beginning as they try to reason out why they got clicked instead of using the click as a marker to give them the vital information to solve the puzzle. At this stage I generally give them a keep going signal so that we can give them further clues (clicks).

To start with the game normally takes a couple of minutes with novice students, but before the session is over the time it takes is around 30 seconds! The training game is usually very instructive and you can see from the audiences' expression if a click was too slow in coming or was missed altogether! An unintentional click can also cause a few gasps of bewilderment.

As a rule there should be no talking during the shaping process, the point of the game is that shaping is a non-verbal interaction. However, cheers, groans, laughter and applause are not only permitted but also are encouraged. The room is quite tense and definitely pulling in the direction of the student subject to get the reinforcable behaviour, and the trainer's complete attention in body and mind is focused on the shaping activity.

When the behaviour has finally been accomplished by mutual agreement with rapturous applause from the audience (this is the reinforcer to the trainer for a job well done).

I always ask how it felt to be the student subject and also what they think the target behaviour was. In some cases the student subject achieved the target behaviour but could not remember the whole process in which they had been involved. Others reported that there was an element of confusion, especially with a novice trainer. Generally the students learn that at the beginning of shaping a subject, more information was better than less.

Generally everyone involved in the Training Game, participants and audience alike, learns from almost every reinforcer (click). The trainer first of all gets to discover what timing is all about and how crucial it is to signal the click while the behaviour is actually occurring. It is clearly obvious, during the exercise in which everyone is participating by agreement and with a will to succeed, that whatever goes wrong is a function of the training, not the trainee subject.

Once you have been the animal subject you will empathise with any animal subject you are training that has not yet fully understood what it is supposed to be doing, so that it easily makes mistakes. So once you have performed the non-verbal shaping with human subjects in an exercise, you may not be so quick to say that the student subject or animal you are training is "plotting revenge" for non-compliance, or "is stupid", or "deliberately trying it on" or "is off colour today" or "is totally untrainable". He or she is just untrained!

Variations of the game

The built in delay: Have three people hold hands. The one at the right hand end of the group is the trainer. When he wants to reinforce the animal he squeezes the middle person's hand; that person squeezes the hand of the third person who then clicks or says "good". Watch what goes wrong with the shaping (by Marian Breland Baily and Robert Bailey).

The group Cheer: Instead of picking one trainer let the whole group cheer and clap when the animal does something deserving of reinforcement and fall silent when the behaviour is not improving. The group can travel around in a building or outdoors, teaching the animal to fetch something from a distance, go over an obstacle, etc. fun for the kids, especially (by Janet Lewis).

In a field or town, at work or rest,
The Dog will always try his best.
As guard and helper, ears and guide
The Dog is with us, there, by our side.

The slipper chewed and carpet torn
Will be forgotten in the morn
When   pleading   eyes   and
trusting paw
Beg forgiveness - just once more.

We say we care, then turn away
From unloved pup and unwanted stray;
Let someone else give them a bed,
Keep them warm, see they are feed.

Yet we should care,
for in the end,
Who can deny that Dog is
man's best friend.

In Conclusion

Thank you for spending some time exploring how dogs learn. How you train, and the method you use, is a reflection of your relationship with your dog. We owe it to our animals to train them in the same way that we would like to be treated. Dogs are incredibly intelligent and have a right to a fun and stimulating environment.

Learning about dogs and their training is an ongoing process; you never know it all, it's a "life time" of steady discovery.

Enjoy your dog, be patient, be calm, be creative, but most of all, have fun with your dog.

Glossary

Antecedent:
>Environmental events that happen before behaviour

Applied Behaviour Analysis:
>The attempt to solve problem behaviour by providing antecedents and/or consequences that change behaviour.

Backward Chaining:
>A chaining procedure that begins with the last element in the chain and progresses to the first element.

Baseline:
>A period during which the target behaviour is monitored, but no attempt is made to change it.

Behaviour:
>Anything a dog does that can be observed.

Behaviour Analysis:
>The science of behaviour change.

Behaviour Assessment:
>The attempt to (1) define the target behaviour. (2) Identify functional relations between target behaviour and its antecedents and consequences. (3) Identify an effective intervention for changing the target behaviour.

Behaviour Repertoire:
>All the things an individual is capable of doing at any given moment.

Chaining:
>The reinforcement of successive elements in a behaviour chain.

Classical Conditioning:
>see Pavlovian conditioning

Conditioned Reinforcers:
>Clickers (secondary reinforcers)

Conditioning:
>see Pavlovian conditioning.

Consequences:
>Environmental events that happen after a behaviour.

Contingency Contract:
>An agreement between two parties about what each is to do

for the other.

Differential Reinforcement:
> Any procedure that combines extinction and reinforcement to change the frequency of the target behaviour.

Discrimination Training:
> Any procedure that results in a target behaviour having different frequencies in different situations.

Discriminative Stimulus:
> Any event in the presence of which a target behaviour is likely to have consequences that effect its frequency. Discriminative stimuli include S^D's (ess-dees) and S$^\Delta$'s (ess-delta's)

DRA (differential reinforcement of alternative behaviour):
> The procedure of reducing the frequency of a target behaviour by reinforcing alternative behaviour. The idea is to give the dog an alternative way of obtaining reinforcers.

DRI (differential reinforcement of incompatible behaviour):
> The procedure of reducing the frequency of the target behaviour by reinforcing a behaviour that is incompatible with the target behaviour.

DRL (differential reinforcement of low rate):
> The procedure of reducing the frequency of the target behaviour by reinforcing it only when it happens at a low rate.

Environmental event:
> Any event in a dog's environment that can be observed.

Escape avoidance learning:
> A learning situation in which the target behaviour results in escape from, or avoidance of an aversive event.

Extinction:
> Withholding the reinforcers that maintain a target behaviour.

Extinction Burst:
> A sharp increase in the frequency of a behaviour that is on extinction. Extinction bursts usually happen soon after behaviour is placed on extinction.

Fading:
> Gradually reducing the strength of a prompt.

Fixed Ratio Schedule:
> A reinforcement schedule in which a reinforcer is provided after the target behaviour has happened n number of times.

Forward Chaining:
> A chaining procedure that begins with the first element in a behaviour chain and progresses to the last element.

Generalisation:
> The tendency for the effects of training to spread.

Law of Effect:
> The principle that, in any given situation, the probability of a

behaviour occurring is a function of the consequences that behaviour has had in that situation in the past. An abbreviated form says that, "behaviour is a function of its consequences"

Learning History:
All the environmental events (antecedents and consequences) that have affected a dog's behaviour up to the present.

Maintenance Schedule:
A reinforcement schedule that maintains a target behaviour at a desired rate.

Maintenance Training:
Intervention procedures that increase the likelihood that changes in target behaviour will persist when the intervention is ended.

Negative Reinforcer:
A reinforcing event in which something is removed following behaviour.

Operant Behaviour:
Behaviour that is readily influenced by events that follow it

Partial Reinforcement Effect (PRE):
The principle that resistance to extinction is greater following intermittent reinforcement than it is following continuous reinforcement.

Pavlovian Conditioning:
Any procedure by which an event comes to elicit a response by being paired with an event that elicits that response.

Positive Reinforcer:
A reinforcing event in which something is added following behaviour.

Primary Reinforcer:
Reinforcers that are not dependent on their association with other reinforcers. (see secondary reinforcers)

Prompt:
An antecedent that induces a dog to perform a behaviour that otherwise would not occur.

Prompting:
The procedure of providing antecedents that evoke a target behaviour.

Punisher:
An event that, when made contingent on a behaviour, decreases the frequency of that behaviour.

Punishment:
The procedure of providing consequences for a behaviour that decreases the frequency of that behaviour.

Ratio Strain:
A reduction in the rate of a target behaviour and an increase

in emotional behaviour resulting from an increase in the ratio of behaviour to reinforcement. (see "stretching the ratio")

Reinforcement:
    The procedure of providing consequences for a behaviour that increase or maintain the frequency of that behaviour.

Reinforcement Schedule:
    see Schedule of reinforcement.

Reinforcer:
    An event that, when made contingent on a behaviour, increases or maintains the frequency of that behaviour.

Respondent Behaviour:
    Behaviour that is most readily influenced by events that precede it; reflexive behaviour.

Response Generalisation:
    The tendency for the effects of training one behaviour to spread to other behaviours.

Reverse chaining:
    see backward chaining.

S^D:
    An event in the presence of which a target behaviour is reinforced

S^Δ:
    An event in the presence of which a target behaviour is not reinforced.

Schedule of Reinforcement:
    A rule governing the delivery of reinforcers.

Secondary Reinforcers:
    Reinforcers that are dependent on their association with other reinforcers. Also called conditioned reinforcers.

Shaping:
    The reinforcement of successive approximations of a target behaviour

Spontaneous Recovery:
    The reappearance of a target behaviour following its extinction.

Stimulus:
    a stimulus is an object or event that can be detected by the senses that can effect a dogs behaviour.

Stimulus Control:
    The tendency for the target behaviour to occur in the presence of a S^D but not in the presence of the S^Δ.

Stimulus Discrimination:
    The tendency for behaviour to have different frequencies in different situations.

Stimulus Generalisation:

The tendency for the effects of training in one situation to spread to other situations.

Stretching The Ratio:

Gradually increasing the number of times behaviour must be performed to qualify for reinforcement.

Target Behaviour:

The behaviour to be changed by an intervention. Usually the goal of an intervention is to change the frequency of a behaviour.

Time Out:

The procedure for reducing the frequency of a target behaviour by making removal of a dog from a reinforcing situation contingent on the target behaviour.

Variable Ratio Schedule:

A reinforcement schedule in which a reinforcer is provided after the target behaviour has occurred a number of times, with the number varying around an average of n.

Bibliography and Resources

Karen Pryor — Don't Shoot the Dog

Murray Sidman — Coercion and its Fallout

James Kopp — Coercion and its Fallout Study Guide

Barry Schwartz & Steven J. Robbins
Psychology of Learning and Behaviour

David A. Lieberman — Learning, Behaviour and Cognition

Mary R. Burch & Jon S. Bailey
How Dogs Learn

Paul Chance — First Course in Applied Behaviour Analysis

Nicky Hayes — Foundation of Psychology

Aubrey Manning & Marion Stamp Dawkins
An Introduction to Animal Behaviour 5th Ed.

Janet R. Lewis — Smart Trainers, Brilliant Dogs

Scott & Fuller — Genetics and the Social Behaviour of the Dog

Dr. Bruce Fogle — The Dog's Mind

Bob & Marion Breland-Bailey
Patients Like the Chipmunks (video)

Useful Addresses

The Association of Pet Dog Trainers
Peacocks Farm
Northchapel
Petworth
West Sussex
GU28 9JB (01428 707620)

The Animal Care College
(Animal behaviour correspondence courses)
Ascot House
High Street
Ascot
Berkshire
SL5 7JG

Crosskeys Select Books
Collier Row Road
Romford
Essex
RM5 2BH

(020 8590 3604) www.Crosskeysbooks.com
For a free catalogue on pet behaviour and training.

The Kennel Club
1, Clarges Street
Piccadilly
London
W1Y 8AB

Index

Website: www.crosskeysbooks.com

Training tips for success

1. Click once, then treat

2. Click as the behaviour happens, if you are teaching your dog to jump, for example, click when the dog is in mid-flight (criteria for height) and for the long jump at the end of the behaviour, just a the dog lands.

3. Never show the dog the rewards (primary reinforcers), let him learn that it is his behaviour that causes the click, which produces the food.

4. Always END practice sessions BEFORE your dog losses interest, so practice sessions should be "short and sweet" of 3-4 minutes, 5 to 6 times per day, in different locations around the house are better than 2 half hour sessions.

5. Watch your dog and capture its natural behaviour; sit, down, stand, come follow me, sniff the ground, head turn, paw lifting, yawn, stretch, shake, play bow, rollover and many more; keep looking, keep clicking!

6. Visualise the whole behaviour and click and treat any small movements in the right direction. If you want the dog to "sit", and it starts to crouch its back end, click.

7. Dogs learn in fits and starts, so go at a pace you both can cope with and remember to start each session with a review of the previous session's behaviour.

8. Good TIMING is everything-if things are not working out you are probably clicking too late, get a training "buddy" to help!

9. Teach in a quiet environment and gradually add distractions: your movements, a friend visiting and then your friend with a friendly dog.

10. What's your dogs MOTIVATION: Use the Canine Reinforcement Analysis.

11. Expect errors, yours and the dog's, behaviour is variable so you will have a second chance to capture your target behaviour.

12. When using the lead, it is there for safety's sake, not as a training tool.

13. Do not rush to add cues/commands until the dog has learned the behaviour. First the dog will learns to sit for a click and treat, Then the dog learns that sitting only gets a click and treat when you say "sit". So that word (cue) becomes a signal that reinforcement is now available for that particular behaviour.

14. When giving a cue/command only give it once and wait until the dog performs the behaviour, then click and treat.

15. Be patient and have fun-if you or your dog are not "up for it", stop, have a cup of coffee and try again later.

16. Mend unwanted behaviour by clicking GOOD behaviour. Click and treat the dog for toileting in the right place. Click for paws on the ground, not on guests.

17. Use the right size of food or treat for your dog. Start your training program before you have fed the dog.

18. Do not fall into the trap of continuous reinforcement, start asking for two behaviours before clicking. (VR)

19. When in doubt, email; info@crosskeysbooks.com for some help. We will try and help you.

20. Above all let your dog see you as a source of all things good, including information about what's safe to do and what's not safe to do, with our clickers. Be creative, have patience and above all have fun.

TO THE OWNER OF THIS BOOK

I hope that you found Ready, Steady, Click! Useful and informative. So that this book can be improved in a future edition, would you take time to complete this sheet and return it? Thank you.

Dog owner/dog training school/Instructors; name and address:

....
....
....

1. What did I like the most about this book:

....
....
....

2. What did I least like about this book:

....
....
....

3. My general reaction to this book is:

....
....
....

4. The name of the course in which I used this book:

....
....

5. Were all the chapters of this book assigned for you to read?

....
....

If not, which ones weren't?

....
....

6. In the space below, or on a separate sheet of paper, please write specific suggestions for improving this book and anything else you would care to share about your experience in using this book:

....
....
....
....

Optional

Your Name:

Date:

May Crosskeys Select Books quote you, either in promotion for Ready, Steady, Click! Or in future publishing ventures?

Yes: ❏   No: ❏

Yours Sincerely

Stephen G. King

.... Fold here ....

<table>
<tr><td></td><td>Stamp
required</td></tr>
</table>

Att. Mr. Stephen G. King
Crosskeys Select Books
Collier Row Road
Romford
Essex
England
RM5 2BH